RELATING DOCTRINE TO DAILY LIFE

An Explanation and Application
of The Basic Doctrines of The Bible

G. Michael Cocoris

© 2010 2025 by G. Michael Cocoris

All rights reserved. This publication may not be reproduced (in whole or in part, edited, or revised) in any way, form, or means, including, but not limited to electronic, mechanical, photocopying, recording, or any kind of storage and retrieval system *for sale*, except for brief quotations in printed reviews, without the written permission of G. Michael Cocoris, 2016 Euclid #20, Santa Monica, CA 90405, michaelcocoris@gmail.com, or his appointed representatives. Permission is hereby granted, however, for the reproduction of the whole or parts of the whole without changing the content in any way for *free distribution*, provided all copies contain this copyright notice in its entirety. Permission is also granted to charge for the cost of copying.

Unless otherwise indicated, all Scripture quotations are taken from the New King James Version ®, Copyright © 1979, 1980, 1982 by Thomas Nelson, Inc. Used by permission. All rights reserved.

Cover design by Victoria Marshall, interior design by John T. Cocoris.

TABLE OF CONTENTS

Preface		
Chapter 1	Know What And Why You believe	1
Chapter 2	What Is God Like?	13
Chapter 3	The Characteristics Of God	23
Chapter 4	The Trinity: The Mind-Blowing Doctrine	37
Chapter 5	What Kind Of Father Is God The Father?	49
Chapter 6	The World's Most Intriguing Person	59
Chapter 7	Life With A Power Assist	71
Chapter 8	Is The Bible The Word Of God?	81
Chapter 9	How To Undertand The Whole Bible	93
Chapter 10	The Biblical View Of You	103
Chapter 11	Sin Is Not What You Think	111
Chapter 12	What Is All This "Salvation" Business	121
Chapter 13	Please Explain Sanctification	131
Chapter 14	What Is The Church?	139
Chapter 15	Toothfaries, Leprechauns, And Angels	153
Chapter 16	An Outline Of Things To Come	165
Chapter 17	What Happens After Death?	177
Chapter 18	What Will Heanve Be Like?	185
Chapter 19	Hell? No!	195
Chapter 20	Definitions, Summary Statements, And Key Passages	203
Chapter 21	How Much Do You Know?	209
About The Author		213

PREFACE

Doctrine. The very word sounds dull and divorced from the practical problems of daily life. Worse yet, discussions of doctrine often degenerate into debate and division. Whole denominations have been formed because of a doctrinal issue.

Doctrine has fallen upon hard times. Its friends have given it bad press. Doctrinal dissertations often major on minors. Doctrinal delineations are sometimes nothing more than hair-splitting. Doctrinal differences result in harsh, judgmental attitudes and actions.

What people today want is something practical. They want something that will help them in their daily life. Most feel that doctrine is neither useful nor helpful.

What is doctrine? Is it practical? Is it possible to relate doctrine to daily life?

The New Testament recognizes a body of truth called doctrine. John speaks about "the doctrine of Christ" (2 Jn. 9). This body of truth is also called "the faith" (Jude 3; Titus 1:13), "the first principles of the oracles of God" (Heb. 5:12) and "elementary principles of Christ" (Heb. 6:1). Throughout the centuries, Christians everywhere have acknowledged a body of truth called doctrine. They have often debated and even divided over this body of truth, but they have all admitted that such a body of truth exists.

The presence of a body of truth, known as doctrine, poses several questions. The first and foremost question is, "What is the content of that body of truth?" Throughout the centuries of church history, various terms have been used to describe accurate doctrine, including orthodox, evangelical, and fundamental.

Creeds and doctrinal statements have been formulated. All of these attempts reflect the issues being debated in their time.

What would the Bible say is the content of the faith once delivered to the saints? That question will be answered in the first chapter. The remaining chapters will explain those various doctrines.

The other major question posed by doctrine concerns value. Is doctrine necessary? To many, doctrine is abstract or philosophical. Hence, it is of little value. Actually, as someone has said, "There is nothing more practical than a good theory." Doctrine, of course, is not theory; it is truth. The point, however, is well taken. The abstract side of doctrine is practical. It provides concepts that determine conduct.

Is doctrine practical? To the average person in the pew, doctrine is unrelated to daily life. It is something that serves to divide. In the Bible, doctrine is *always* practical. Doctrine and daily life go together like peanut and jelly, salt and pepper, and sand and beach. The purpose of this material is not only to expound the doctrines of the Christian faith but to relate them to daily life. Each chapter will demonstrate how doctrine relates to life.

I am grateful to Gladys Watchulonis, who proofread the original material of this book, and to Teresa Rogers, who proofread this edition, which contains some revisions.

I pray that the Lord will use these studies to enable you to understand the basic doctrinal teachings of the Scripture clearly and to implement them in your daily life.

G. Michael Cocoris
Santa Monica, California

CHAPTER 1

KNOW WHAT YOU BELIEVE AND WHY

Have you ever talked to someone who believes something different than you concerning something in the Bible and after the conversation, you thought to yourself, "I wish I knew my Bible as well as he or she does?" Have you ever had that experience and thought to yourself, "Now I'm confused; I'm not sure what I believe?" Have you ever wondered if what you believe about something in the Bible is correct? Would you like to become spiritually mature? The solution to all these problems is doctrine. What is doctrine? Why do we need it and how can it help us?

Doctrine Is Biblical Beliefs

The Apostles' Doctrine The Scripture speaks of doctrine. For example, when Peter preached on the day of Pentecost, 3,000 people were converted. Luke then says, "And they continued steadfastly in the apostles' doctrine in fellowship and in the breaking of bread and in prayers" (Acts 2:42). The Greek word translated "doctrine" means "teaching, instruction." It was used of the act of teaching or what is taught.

What is the content of the apostles' doctrine? What did they teach? Acts 2 does not answer that question, but the answer is obvious. Under the direction of the Holy Spirit, the apostles wrote instructions to individuals and churches (2 Pet. 1:20-21). In other words, the apostles' doctrine is the New Testament (2 Tim. 3:16). The whole New Testament is doctrine, that is, teaching, but that teaching can be divided into two types. There is a teaching in the New Testament that could be called "beliefs." Those beliefs exist apart from behavior. There is also a teaching in the New Testament that is behavioral. John speaks of the doctrine of Christ (2 Jn. 9). Apart from what anyone does, there is a teaching about Christ. On the other hand, Paul tells slaves to adorn the doctrine of God (Titus 2:10). That kind of teaching is behavioral; thus, doctrine can be divided into beliefs and behaviors. There are philosophical doctrines and practical doctrines.

The Faith: There are other indications in the New Testament of a body of truth referred to as doctrine, which encompasses a set of beliefs. For example, Jude mentions "the faith that was once for all delivered to the saints" (Jude 3). The expression "the faith" implies a body of truth that is to be believed. The question is, "What is the content of the doctrines to be believed, the philosophical doctrines?" The Bible does not list all of these doctrines in one place. There is no doctrinal statement in the Scripture!

To complicate matters, when believers have formulated doctrinal pronouncements throughout church history, it has been a reaction to the denial of a doctrine. Christians were forced to articulate what they believed the Scriptures taught. In the early centuries, Christians wrote creeds, that is, doctrinal statements, concerning the Trinity and the person of Christ, because of controversies over these subjects.

The Doctrine of Christ Apart from some denial or debate, what does the New Testament teach about the content of the doctrines to be believed? The expressions of doctrinal beliefs in the New Testament, along with their context, provide an answer to this question.

The expression "the doctrine of Christ" as used by John (2 Jn. 9) is the belief that Jesus is the Christ, the Son of God come in the flesh (see also 1 Jn. 2:22; 4:2). The doctrine of Christ implies the Trinity. If Jesus is the Son, there is a Father. The doctrinal content of the New Testament, at the very least, includes teachings about God, the Trinity, and the Person of Christ.

There is more. In 2 Corinthians, the apostle Paul speaks about false apostles (2 Cor. 11:13), who were preaching another Jesus, a different Spirit, and a different gospel (2 Cor. 11:4). This verse indicates that the doctrinal content that concerns Paul included not only teachings about Christ and the Holy Spirit but about the gospel as well. The inclusion of teachings about the gospel implies teachings about people and their relationship with God. The gospel states that Christ died for our sins and rose from the dead (1 Cor. 15:3-4). The gospel is predicated on the teaching that people are made in the image of God, are sinful, and need a Savior. It also implies teachings about repentance and faith.

In other words, the Bible is a book about God. It has a great deal to say about His nature and activities. Equally obvious, the Bible has much to say about people. It records their creation, fall into sin, and focuses on their relationship with God and others, all of which stem from their relationship with God.

In its simplest form, the doctrine ("the faith") consists of three basic things: 1) teachings about God, 2) teachings about people, and 3) teachings about relationships between the two. More specifically, the doctrine includes teachings about the Trinity (God the Father, God the Son, and God the Holy Spirit), the sinfulness of humans, and the gospel.

A seminary student once told me he was taking a course on the theology of an Old Testament book. When I asked him what that meant, he said that the professor suggested that theology consisted of truth about God, truth about people, and truth about the relationship between the two. The class reviewed Old Testament books, picking out what they said about those three areas. In its most basic form, that's doctrine.

First Principles The New Testament would also include other subjects. In Hebrews 6, the writer to the Hebrews mentions "the elementary principles of Christ" and lists six doctrines, namely, repentance, faith, the doctrine of baptisms, the laying on of hands, the resurrection of the dead, and eternal judgment (Heb. 6:1-2). Repentance and faith are gospel truths. The doctrines of baptism and the laying on of hands used in ordination are church truths. The future resurrection and the judgments that follow are prophetic truths. Therefore, from this passage, it could be concluded that the doctrinal content of the New Testament includes salvation truth, church truth, and prophetic truth. In a sense, these truths still fit the three basic categories. After all, people relate to God in the church and the future.

To sum up, from the New Testament point of view, the content of doctrine includes the categories of 1) the Godhead, including the Father, the Son, and the Holy Spirit, with a particular focus on the person and work of Christ, 2) the nature and need of people, 3) salvation, 4) the church, and 5) future things. Theologians have given these doctrinal areas technical names: 1) theology proper, 2) anthropology, 3) soteriology, 4) ecclesiology, and 5) eschatology.

These topics are the content of "belief" or "doctrine" in the New Testament. These are the subjects covered in books on doctrine and theology. One theology book is divided into twelve parts. The titles of those parts are 1) studying God, 2) knowing God, 3) what is God like, 4) what God does, 5) humanity, 6) sin, 7) the person of Christ,

8) the work of Christ, 9) the Holy Spirit, 10) salvation, 11) the church, and 12) last things. Other theologies may divide doctrines slightly differently, but although the divisions are different, the content of the areas of theology is basically the same, and they reflect what the New Testament teaches as doctrine.

Everyone has a doctrine, a creed, beliefs. The Lone Ranger Creed was once as familiar to boys in America as the Boy Scout Oath. Fran Striker wrote it as the kind of creed that felt good. It read:

I believe...
That to have a friend, a man must be one.
That all men are created equal and that everyone has within himself the power to make this a better world.
That God put the firewood there, but that every man must gather and light it himself.
That a man should be prepared physically, mentally, and morally to fight when necessary for that which is right.
That a man should make the most of what equipment he has.
That "this government, of the people, by the people, and for the people" shall live always.
That men should live by the rule of what is best for the greatest number.
That sooner or later—somewhere, somehow—we must settle with the world and make payment for what we have taken.
That all things change, but truth and that truth alone lives on forever.
I believe in my Creator, my country, and my fellow man.

The Little League Pledge is:

> I trust in God
> I love my country
> And will respect its laws
> I will play fair
> And strive to win
> But win or lose, I will always do my best

Your beliefs should be biblical. Why should you have biblical doctrine?

Doctrine Prevents Deception and Instability

Deception Yes, an emphatic yes! There are many ways doctrine is related to daily life. Two are particularly important. First, doctrine prevents deception. John says there are anti-Christs and false prophets in the world trying to deceive believers (1 Jn. 2:26, 2:18-19; 4:1). The issue he had in mind was the doctrine of Christ (1 Jn. 2:21-22; 4:1-3). Believers knew the truth (1 Jn. 2:21). He did not want them deceived (1 Jn. 2:26) by a lie (1 Jn. 2:22; 4:6).

Paul had a similar concern. He warned the Corinthians about false apostles, people he called deceitful workers (2 Cor. 11:13). He feared that the Corinthians would be deceived (2 Cor. 11:3). The issues he had in mind were the doctrines of Christ, the Holy Spirit, and the gospel (2 Cor. 11:4).

How does that relate to daily life? Some Tuesday morning or Thursday afternoon, your doorbell will ring, and when you open the door, you will meet two well-mannered people who want you to read their literature. They will tell you that Jesus is not deity and that to be related to God, you must work. At that point, doctrine relates to your daily life.

Spiritual Instability Deception produces spiritual instability. Paul said all believers need to come to the unity of the faith (Eph. 4:13) so they would not be deceived and thus tossed to and fro and carried about by every wind of doctrine (Eph. 4:14). When believers do not know doctrine, they are immature, unstable, and susceptible to every new thing that comes along. They will be tossed to and fro.

Don't be like a leaf in the wind. Be stable like a boulder. "In matters of style, swim with the current; in matters of principle, stand like a rock" (Thomas Jefferson).

Let me illustrate. No less than Paul taught the Thessalonians the doctrine of prophecy (1 Thess. 4:13-18), but they did not learn that doctrine thoroughly enough. Someone came along to give them some false information and some of the Thessalonians quit their jobs (2 Thess. 3:11). Paul said to them, "Now brethren, concerning the coming of our Lord Jesus Christ and our gathering together to Him, we ask you not to be soon shaken in minor trouble either by spirit or by word or by letter as if from us, as though the day of Christ had come. Let no one deceive you by any means" (2 Thess. 2:1-3). Notice carefully: the Thessalonians had received false information concerning the coming of Christ (2 Thess. 2:1). They were in danger of being deceived by it (2 Thess. 2:3) and, as a result, were shaken and troubled (2 Thess. 2:2). Some of the Thessalonians quit their jobs (2 Thess. 3:11). Their deception and disorderly behavior were related. Because they thought they were in the Tribulation, they quit their jobs! Their deception led to instability.

A cartoon says it well. Pastor Wilkins sat behind his desk, a look of utter disbelief upon his face. Standing in front of him was church member Mrs. Trent. "According to my horoscope," she said, "this is a good week to preach against false doctrine."

Doctrine is Necessary for Maturity

There is a second major way that doctrine relates to daily life. Doctrine is essential for spiritual maturity.

Doctrine is Necessary The writer to the Hebrews called his original readers babes and said they needed milk (Heb. 5:12) and milk is for babes (Heb. 5:13). In other words, they needed "the first principles" (Heb. 5:12). He calls these first principles the "elementary principles of Christ" (Heb. 6:1) and identifies six of them (Heb. 6:1-2), which include the doctrines of salvation, the church, and prophecy.

Notice he says they needed these (Heb. 5:12) and they need to leave these (Heb. 6:1). Is that a contradiction? No. He calls these first principles "the foundation" (Heb. 6:1). He does not mean to leave them like leaving or forsaking one city to travel to another. He means to leave them like a contractor would leave the foundation of a building to put the superstructure on top of it. You need to build on the foundation, which means you need the foundation and more. Doctrine is necessary for spiritual maturity.

Let's be specific. Can you answer questions in these six areas? 1) What is the meaning of repentance? 2) What is the meaning of faith? 3) How many baptisms are there in the New Testament, and what are they? 4) What is the meaning and the use of the laying on of hands? 5) How many resurrections are there? Who is involved in each one, and when will each one take place? 6) How many judgments are there? Who is involved in each one, and when will each one take place? You are at least a babe if you can answer these questions correctly! If you can't, you need to be taught the first principles.

Experience is also Necessary You must have doctrine, but doctrine alone is not enough. You must have experience too (Heb. 5:14). It is by using doctrine that one reaches spiritual maturity over time. The point is that to reach maturity, one needs to understand the elementary principles and live accordingly.

That which is true spiritually is true in other areas as well. The study of any subject in any field begins with defining terms and describing concepts. For example, if you were to study psychology at a university, you would have to start by taking a course entitled "The Introduction to Psychology." In that course, you would be introduced to psychological terms and concepts such as stress, anxiety, defense mechanisms, neurosis, psychosis, etc. To help students understand the concepts of defense mechanisms, the teacher would explain rationalization, projection, repression, and suppression, among others.

The same is true of other fields of endeavor. People wishing to study auto mechanics typically attend a trade school, where they begin with the basics. They would have to learn terms such as carburetor, alternator, and transmission. They would have to understand concepts like the workings of the internal combustion engine.

In other words, to be a mature counselor or mechanic, one must learn and practice the field's basic concepts. Rushing into counseling or mechanics without understanding the basic principles of the field will lead to disastrous results. If people are to ever mature in either of those fields or any other, they must, at some point, master the basics.

Maturing spiritually is precisely the same as studying any other subject. One must understand terms and concepts. These terms include such biblical words as sin, repentance, faith, the gospel, redemption, reconciliation, propitiation, the cross of Christ, the body of Christ, the coming of Christ, etc. Behind each of these terms is a concept that must be mastered. Then, that concept must be implemented in one's life.

"Nothing makes a man so virtuous as belief of the truth. A lying doctrine will soon beget a lying practice. A man cannot have an erroneous belief without by-and-by having an erroneous life. I believe one naturally begets the other" (Charles Haddon Spurgeon). "Too much of our orthodoxy is correct and sound, but like words without a tune, it does not glow and burn; it does not stir the heart; it has lost its hallelujah. One man with a genuine glowing experience with God is worth a library full of arguments" (Vance Havner, *Leadership*, vol. 15, no. 3).

Summary: Believers must know doctrine to prevent deception and instability and to be spiritually mature.

You need to know doctrine. Many believers react negatively to the word doctrine, but the questions they ask necessitate understanding doctrine to answer. For over 60 years, I have conducted hundreds of question-and-answer sessions for teenagers and adults. In all of those years, I cannot recall having a single question-and-answer session that lasted for any time, but one or more doctrinal questions were not asked. When you begin to ask questions about the Christian faith, whether you know it or not, you are asking doctrinal questions. The truth is, you must know to grow.

As you read your Bible, you need to note what it says about the five major areas of doctrine: God, people, salvation, the church, and the future. Why not start a notebook? Begin with one page per subject. Begin to write down what you believe about those subjects, where you can prove that from the Bible, and what difference it makes in your daily life.

To put the whole thing another way, if you don't know what to believe, you don't know what to do. The story is about a gang of boys who raided a farmer's watermelon patch. A neighbor suggested that to prevent future raids, the farmer needed to place a sign at the edge of the field reading, "One watermelon in this patch is poison." The next day, when the boys saw the farmer leave for the market, they headed for his watermelon patch. They were shocked when they read the sign.

Just as they were about to leave, an idea popped into the mind of one of them. Reaching deep into his pocket, he produced a piece of chalk and altered the part of the message on the sign. When he was finished, it read, "Two watermelons in this patch are poison." When the farmer returned, he found himself in a predicament. Not knowing whether to believe the sign and not knowing which of the watermelons might have been contaminated, he didn't know what to do.

You must know what to believe so you can know how to behave.

CHAPTER 2

WHAT IS GOD LIKE?

An overwhelming number of people believe that there is a God. Years ago, the Gallup Poll conducted a worldwide survey concerning God and religion. They asked, "Do you believe in the existence of God or a supernatural spirit?" At the time, 98% of the interviewees in India answered in the affirmative, as did 96% of those in sub-Saharan Africa. 95% of Latin Americans answered, "Yes," while 94% of Americans replied positively. This compares with 89% in Canada, 88% in Italy, 78% in Western Europe, and only 38% in Japan.

Years later, polls indicated that the percentages were not as high in some countries, but the overwhelming majority still claimed to believe in God. In 2012, the Pew Research Center's Forum on Religion & Public Life said a comprehensive demographic study of more than 230 countries and territories revealed that "Worldwide, more than eight-in-ten people identify with a religious group." A July 2025 Gallup poll reported that 71% believed in God and 10% were atheists.

When it comes to specifics, there are vast differences. Primitive people describe God as an image, statue, or idol. Some civilized people define God as a "force" or "power." Immanuel Kant reduced God to a subjective sentiment. Friedrich Nietzsche declared that God was dead. Charles Darwin found chance a better explanation for the cosmos than a Creator. Karl Marx believed that God was the "opiate of the masses" invented by the ruling classes. Sigmund Freud insisted that God was merely a neurosis.

What, then, is God like? An exhaustive description of God cannot be given in one sermon, book, or lifetime. Only eternity can even begin to do justice to that job. Nevertheless, from the data revealed in the Scriptures, some basic statements can be made concerning the nature of God.

God is a Person

God is not a force, influence, or power; He is a person. Having said that, what has been said? What is a person?

Theology Theologians define "person" as "a being with a mind, emotions, and a will." Lewis Sperry Chafer said: "Those elements which combine to form personality are intellect, sensibility, and will.... Intellect must direct, sensibility must desire and will must determine the direction of rational ends. There can be no personality, either human, angelic or divine, apart from this complex of essentials" (Lewis Sperry Chafer, *Systematic Theology*, vol. 1, p. 185).

A Bible teacher put it like this: "Personality exists where there is intellect, mind, will, reason, individuality, self-consciousness, and self-determination. There must not be mere consciousness—for the beasts have that—but self-consciousness" (William Evans, *Great Doctrines of the Bible,* p. 22). R. A. Torrey wrote, "Personality is characterized by knowledge, feeling and will" (R. A. Torrey, *What the Bible Teaches*, p. 26).

Scripture The Bible represents God as a person. In Genesis 1, He creates, which takes a mind and a will. In Genesis 3, He communicates, which takes a mind and a will. What about emotion? To see all three of the basic elements of personhood in

God, consider Genesis 6:5-7, which says: "Then the Lord saw that the wickedness of man was great in the earth and that every intent of the thought of the heart was only evil continually. And the Lord was sorry that He made man on the earth and He was grieved in His heart, so the Lord said, "I will destroy man whom I have created on the face of the earth, both man and beast, creeping thing and birds of the air, for I am sorry that I have made them" (Gen. 6:5-7).

This passage reveals that God has a mind. He saw wickedness. What He saw was a material object and a mental perception: wickedness. The Lord has emotion; He was sorry (Gen. 6:6). He also has a will, for He said, "I will destroy man" (Gen. 6:7). Throughout the Bible, God is referred to by the personal pronoun "I," "You," and "Him," not "it."

To underscore the personhood of God, look at Jeremiah 10:1-16, where Jeremiah contrasts the living God with the idols of his day. He points out that the gods of the Gentiles were nothing more than a carving from a tree (Jer. 10:3-4). Those idols were indeed not persons (Jer. 10:5). In contrast to dead idols, "The Lord is the true God; He is the living God and the everlasting King" (Jer. 10:10). The expression "living God" is used elsewhere in the Scripture to emphasize that God is a person, not a thing (also Acts 14:15; 1 Thess. 1:9).

Though there is idol worship in primitive and uncivilized places in the world today, the Christians in America are more likely to meet the pantheism of the New Age Movement, which says that God is everything and everything is God; God is all, all is God. Thus, God is not held to be independent and separate from nature. He is reduced to an unconscious force in the world. The Bible, on the other hand, teaches that God is a Person. He is not the world; He made the world.

Implications In his *Systematic Theology*, Berkhof said, "It is, of course, of the greatest importance to maintain the personality of God for without it there can be no religion in the real sense of the word: no prayer, no personal communion, no truthful reliance, no confident hope" (L. Berkhof, *Systematic Theology*, p. 84). Because God is a person, He can act, and an individual today can know Him and communicate with Him.

Even believers in Jesus Christ can forget that God is a Person. We sometimes reduce Christianity to rules and regulations. It's bad enough when we make a list of do's. It's worse when we make a list of don'ts. The do's include going to church, reading your Bible, praying, witnessing, and giving money. The don'ts are the filthy five, the terrible ten, and the dirty dozen (drinking, smoking, dancing, playing cards, going to movies, etc.). Christianity includes some do's and don'ts, but it is a relationship with a Person first and foremost.

Let me illustrate. Marriage is primarily a relationship with a person, but it can be reduced to rules and regulations such as, "You must kiss your wife goodbye every morning." Now, there is certainly nothing wrong with kissing your wife every morning, but when rules regulate the relationship, it becomes mechanical. If the personal relationship is maintained, the kissing will take care of itself. If we remember God is a Person and we relate to Him personally, the rules and regulations will take care of themselves.

God is a Spirit

God is a Spirit The second basic thing that can be said about God is that He is a Spirit. The classic statement of that truth fell from the lips of Christ as He engaged a Samaritan woman in conversation.

The contrast between the two of them was dramatic. He was a man; she was a woman. He was a Jew; she was a Samaritan. The Jews and the Samaritans hated each other. There was as much racial tension between them as between Jews and Arabs in the Middle East, the Blacks and the Whites in the South, and Protestants and Catholics in Northern Ireland, but the biggest contrast was religion.

The Jews said God dwelt in Jerusalem in Mount Zion. The Samaritans said that He dwelt in Mount Gerizim. During their conversation, when they got to the issue of God, the Samaritan woman brought up the differences between the Jewish and Samaritan concepts of God. In reply, Jesus indicated that both were wrong. He said, "God is Spirit and those who worship Him must worship Him in Spirit and in truth" (Jn. 4:24).

Spirits do not have bodies. What does that mean? What is a spirit? Again, a statement, which comes from the teachings of Christ, is helpful here. After His resurrection, He appeared to the disciples who were terrified, thinking they had seen a spirit (Lk. 24:37). Today, we would say they thought they had seen a ghost. At any rate, in response, Jesus said, "A spirit does not have flesh and bones as you see I have" (Lk. 24:39). By flesh and bones, He meant a body. So, saying God is a spirit is saying He does not have a body. In other words, God is invisible (Col. 1:15; Heb. 11:27). He has nothing of a material or bodily nature.

Does the Bible not say God's hand is not shortened so that He cannot save, nor is His ear so heavy that He cannot hear (Isa. 59:1)? Does this not prove that God has a body? The answer is "No." The Bible says that God has hands, feet, arms, eyes, and ears and that He sees, feels, hears, and walks. That does not mean, however, that He has a body. Such descriptions are human expressions bringing the infinite within the comprehension of the finite. They are figures of speech. Theologians call them anthropomorphisms. The Greek word "anthropo" means "man" and "morphism" is Greek for "form." Thus, this compound Greek word means "to attribute human form to." This is a case of "body language" with no body!

Walter Martin was lecturing on this subject when a cultist stood up in the question and answer session and quoted passages of Scripture that refer to God as having human body parts to prove that God had a body. He said, for example, "Underneath are the Everlasting Arms, My eyes are not closed that I cannot see, My ears are not stopped that I cannot hear, your feasts are a stench in My nostrils, His head of hair is as white as wool, His feet are planted in the footsteps of the deep."

Martin listened patiently and replied, "But Psalm 91:4 says, 'He shall cover you with His feathers, and under His wing, you shall take refuge.' God, then, is a chicken!" He went on to say that the book of Hebrews says, 'God is a consuming fire.' Does that mean that God is a blast furnace? Jesus said, 'I am the door.' Does that mean He has wood hinges, a handle, and a knocker? Of course not! These are figures of speech."

The fact that God is a spirit and not a thing means that He can be worshipped anywhere, not just on Mount Zion and Mount Gerizim. Though believers know better, they often treat God like He is an object located in one spot. They only relate to Him through the rites and rituals of the church. They forget Him or neglect Him during the day. It is as if He is handcuffed to the pulpit in the church. God is Spirit, which means that we can relate to Him everywhere.

God is Eternal

Scripture The next basic thing that could be said about God is that He is eternal. Moses wrote, "The Eternal God is your refuge and underneath are the Everlasting Arms" (Deut. 33:27). Paul states, "Now to the King Eternal, immortal, invisible, to God, who alone is wise be honor and glory forever and ever. Amen" (1 Tim. 1:17).

Explanation The word "eternal" is used in two different senses. Figuratively, it means an existence that has a beginning but will have no end. Angels and humans are in this class of beings. Humans have a birthday, a beginning day, and will die. Yet, they do not have an end day. They live forever in eternity.

The other way "eternal" is used is in the literal sense to refer to an existence that has neither beginning nor end. God is in that category. Psalm 90:2 says, "Before the mountains were brought forth, or You ever had formed the earth and the world, even from everlasting to everlasting, You are God."

Children often ask, "Where did God come from?" The answer is, "He always was." A deaf-mute pupil in the Institute of Paris expressed his idea of the eternality of deity when he wrote, "It is duration without beginning or end; existence, without bonds or dimensions; present, without past or future. His eternity is youth without infancy or old age; life without birth or death; today, without yesterday or tomorrow."

Since God is eternal, we can have a relationship with Him forever. Many human relationships do not last long. People change jobs or move. Even the closest of human relationships, marriage, sometimes ends in divorce. Because God is eternal and made us so that we can live forever, we can have an eternal relationship with Him.

Summary: God is an eternal, spiritual person (1 Tim. 1:17).

Since God is a person, we can know Him, not just have an impersonal knowledge about Him. Someone has pointed out that an impersonal knowledge of God is like the tail feathers of a peacock, highly ornamental but not of much use in a windstorm. Like Paul, the passion of our heart should be "that I may know Him and the power of His resurrection, and the fellowship of His sufferings, being conformed to His death" (Phil. 3:10). Get to know Him as the Judge (Ps. 75:7), who is righteous, the King (Ps. 74:12), who is sovereign, and the Shepherd (Ps. 80:1), who cares.

Since God is spirit, a person's knowledge of God is spiritual. Knowledge of God is not obtained by physical means. La Place swept the heavens with his telescope but could not find God anywhere. He might just as well have swept a kitchen with a broom. Since God is eternal, it is possible not only to know Him now but to know Him forever and ever.

Get to know the Lord, not for His blessing or for His benefits, but just for Him. Get to know Him, not just as a rescuer, provider, and protector, but as a person. A. B. Simpson wrote:

NOW IT IS THE LORD

Once it was a blessing,
Now it is the Lord;
Once it was the feeling,
Now it is His Word.
Once His gifts I wanted,
Now the Giver own;
Once I sought for healing,
Now Himself alone.

Once 'twas painful trying,
Now 'tis perfect trust;
Once a half salvation,
Now that uttermost.
Once was ceaseless holding,
Now He holds me fast;
Once 'twas constant drifting,
Now my anchor's cast.
Once 'twas busy planning,
Now 'tis trustful prayer;
Once 'twas anxious caring,
Now He has the care.
Once 'twas what I wanted,
Now what Jesus says;
Once 'twas constant asking,
Now 'tis ceaseless praise.

Once it was my working,
His it hence shall be;
Once I tried to use Him,
Now He uses me.
Once the power I wanted,
Now the Mighty one;
Once for self I labored,
Now for Him alone.

Once I hoped in Jesus,
Now I know He's mine;
Once my lamps were dying,
Now they brightly shine.
Once for death I waits,
Now His coming hail;
And my hopes are anchored,
Safe within the veil.

CHAPTER 3

THE CHARACTERISTICS OF GOD

When my mother and father were divorced, my father didn't just move out of the house; he moved out of town. I was only six years old at the time. After that, I only saw him once or twice a year and then only briefly. He died when I was fourteen. I knew my father in the sense that "I met him," but I never knew him in the sense of getting to know him. So, as an adult, I have asked my mother and others, "What was my father like?"

Many Christians know their Heavenly Father in that they have met Him through His Son, Jesus Christ, but they do not know Him in the sense of knowing what He is like. They should ask, "What is my Father like?"

When I asked that question concerning my earthly father, I was given a list of characteristics. For example, he was hardworking, generous, and had a sense of humor. When Christians ask what God is like, they are usually given a list of characteristics. Theologians call these characteristics attributes. For example, God is sovereign, omnipresent, immutable, omniscient, omnipotent, holy, righteous, loving, gracious, etc. The list is long. That's a problem. The tendency with a long list is to want to divide it. The question is, "how?"

The characteristics of humans are divided into two categories: good and bad. Such a division will not work with the characteristics of God. How, then are the attributes of God to be characterized?

Interestingly, all theologians divide God's attributes into two categories. They differ, however, on what the two categories should be and what these categories should be called.

Some use the divisions of absolute and relative: absolute belonging to the essence of God and relative belonging to the essence of God considered in relationship to His creation. This assumes that we have some knowledge of God, as He is in Himself, apart from His relation to His creatures. That, of course, is not so. Technically, all God's attributes indicate that He is in relationship to His creatures so all of His attributes are relative.

Others use the categories of natural and moral, referring to God's constitutional nature apart from His will and moral, indicating God's moral being. The objection to this division is that moral attributes are natural.

The most common distinction is between incommunicable and communicable. The incommunicable attributes of God are those characteristics that are incapable of being communicated. These are in God alone; there is nothing analogous in human beings. Communicable attributes, on the other hand, are capable of being communicated. These are found, at least to some degree, in humans. The problem with this approach is that all of God's attributes are communicable to some degree.

All methods of dividing God's characteristics into categories break down. After all, we're dealing with God. Because it is the most common, the last-mentioned method will be followed.

Incommunicable Attributes

Sovereignty God is sovereign; that is, He is supreme. He rules over everything. God has absolute authority. He is the boss. The

Scripture puts it like this, "Yours, Oh Lord, is the greatness, the power and the glory, the victory and the majesty; for all that is in heaven and in earth is yours; yours is the kingdom, Oh Lord, and You are exalted as head over all. Both riches and honor come from You, and You reign over all. In your hand is power and might; in your hand, it is to make great and to give strength to all" (1 Chron. 29:11-12).

The mayor has authority over a city, but there is a higher authority than that. A governor has authority over a state, but there is an authority higher than that. The citizens of the United States recognize the president as the highest authority in the country, yet they realize his power is limited. God is the ultimate authority and He has no limits. There is no other authority outside of Him.

That means, among other things, that all things belong to God. First Chronicles 29:11 says, "All that is in heaven and in earth" belongs to God. Chafer wrote: "He is Creator and His dominion is perfect and final...All material things are His by the most absolute ownership. Men hold property by rights which are only temporary and permitted by God (Psalm 50:10)."

God's sovereignty also means that He rules as king in the most absolute sense of the word. First Chronicles 29:12 says, "You reign over all." Just as He allows men the temporal right for property, yet He is the ultimate and absolute owner, so He allows others, both Satan and men, to make choices, but He is the ultimate and absolute arbitrator of the universe.

God is God! The first and foremost thing that can be said about what God is like is He is God. People often do not like that; they hate it. They want to whittle God down. However, no matter what people say or do, God is still God.

Omnipresence God is omnipresent. "Omni" means "all;" thus omnipresent means "all present" or "everywhere present." How can that be? Remember, this is an incommunicable attribute. These types of characteristics cannot be communicated absolutely. Yet God is indeed everywhere present.

The psalmist said, "Where can I go from Your spirit, or where can I flee from Your presence? If I ascend into heaven, You are there. If I make my bed in hell, behold, You are there. If I take the wings of the morning and dwell in the uttermost part of the sea, even there, Your hand shall lead me and Your right hand shall hold me. If I say, 'surely the darkness shall fall on me,' even the night shall be light about me. Indeed, the darkness shall not hide from You, but the light shines as the day. The darkness and the light are both alike to You" (Ps. 139:7-12).

Candidly, this is a tricky truth. God is a person and, as such, is in a place. In the Lord's Prayer, we are told to pray, "Our Father in heaven" (Mt. 6:9). At the same time, God is a spirit and, as such, is everywhere. It's a tricky truth. Be that as it may, the fact remains that God is everywhere present. His center is everywhere; His circumference is nowhere. God is everywhere; there is no place He is not.

Having said that, it needs to be added that He is not everywhere present in the same sense, but He is everywhere present. The presence is spiritual, not material. Yet, it is a real presence. This aspect of the omnipresence of God has been compared to the omnipresence of a speaker in a large auditorium. In one sense, he's on the platform behind the podium. Yet, in another sense, he is omnipresent in that he is everywhere present. Yet he is not everywhere present in the same sense.

Practically, the omnipresence of God means two things. It is a protective truth and it is a detective truth. It is protective in that God is with every believer. That is a great comfort. As Feber has said, "Speak to Him, then, for He listens. And spirit with spirit can meet; closer is He than breathing, nearer than hand or feet. God is never so far off as ever to be near; He is within. Our spirit is the home He holds most dear. To think of Him as by our side is almost as untrue as to remove His shrine beyond those skies of starry blue."

The omnipresence of God is also a detective truth. You can never escape God. You can never get out of His knowledge. You can never get out of His sight. You can never get out of His presence. That alone should keep you from sin.

In short, you can never talk about God behind His back.

Immutability God is immutable. To be mutable means "capable of change." Thus, to be immutable is to be unchangeable. God Himself said, "For I am the Lord, I do not change" (Mal. 3:6).

God is perfect. Perfection doesn't need to change. As one teenager jokingly said to the other, "I am perfect; it's hard to improve on perfection." Seriously, coming from a human, that's pride. Coming from God, it's the plain truth.

God's person is immutable. He is sovereign and that never changes. He is omnipresent and that remains the same. Immutability also applies to God's promises. He says, "Believe on the Lord Jesus Christ and you will be saved." Imagine someone saying, "God, I admit I'm a sinner. I acknowledge Christ died for my sins and here and now, I trust Jesus Christ to save me." Then suppose God said, "I'm sorry, that was yesterday's deal, now today I've changed my mind. Today's conditions are...." Because God is immutable, such a conversation will never take place.

Immutability, however, does not apply to God's program. He does change that. His program in the Old Testament centered around the Tabernacle and sacrifices. In the New Testament, it changed. The church became God's program.

Some quote the verse, "Jesus Christ is the same yesterday, today and forever" (Heb. 13:8) to prove that what God did in the New Testament times He does today (healing), but the immutability of God applies to His Person and His promises, not necessarily to His programs. A simple reading of the Bible indicates that God has changed His program through the ages.

Communicable Attributes

Omniscience God is omniscient; He knows all things. The apostle John wrote, "For if our heart condemns us, God is greater than our heart and knows all things" (1 Jn. 3:20). God's omniscience includes all things actual and all things possible (Mt. 11:21-22).

Just before Christmas break, an ill-prepared college student wrote on an exam paper, "Only God knows the answers to these questions. Merry Christmas." When the professor graded the paper, he wrote a note that read, "God gets 100; you get 0. Happy New Year." Regarding knowledge, God gets 100—one hundred percent of the time. Has it ever occurred to you that nothing has ever occurred to God?

This truth can be used to convict, which is how most preachers and teachers use it. God is watching; God knows, so beware. It is like a prison cell with one small hole with a guard watching the prisoner day and night. All the prisoners can see is the guard's eye, but the eye is always there. Day and night, he always sees the eye when he looks up. There's no hiding. There's no escape.

When he lies down and rises up, the eye is always watching. If a person had something to hide, the all-seeing eye of God would definitely be a source of irritation.

Social scientists know that people begin behaving differently once they realize they are being observed.

The omniscience of God is also a comforting truth. God knows and God cares. He knows, so I don't have to worry. During World War II, the King of England ordered the evacuation of all children from the bomb-torn areas of London. Many of those youngsters had never been away from home before and thus were very nervous and upset. A father and mother put their young son and daughter aboard a crowded train and said goodbye. The little girl began to cry as soon as the train pulled away from the station. She told her brother she was scared because she didn't know where they were going. Brushing her tears away, the older brother put his arm around his little sister to comfort her: "I don't know where we're going either," he said, "but the king knows, so don't worry."

God has never said, "I wish I had known," or "If I had known, I would have done it another way."

Ryrie says, "The practical ramifications of the omniscience of God are many. Think, for instance, what this means in relation to the eternal security of the believer. If God knows all, then obviously nothing can come to light subsequent to our salvation, which He did not know when He saved us. There were no skeletons in the closet, which He did not know about when He offered to give us eternal salvation. Think again about what omniscience means when something tragic occurs in our lives. God knows and has known all about it from the beginning and is working all things out for His glory and our ultimate good. Consider what omniscience ought to mean in relation to living the Christian life. Here is

Someone who knows all the pitfalls as well as the ways to be happy and who has offered to give us this wisdom. If we would heed what He says, then we could avoid a lot of trouble and experience a lot of happiness" (Charles C. Ryrie, *A Survey of Bible Doctrine*, p. 18).

Omnipotence God is also omnipotent, which, of course, means God has all power. The last book of the Bible says, "And I heard, as it were, the voice of a great multitude, as the sound of many waters and as the sound of mighty thunderings, saying, 'Alleluia! For the Lord God Omnipotent reigns!'" (Rev. 19:6). To be more concise, the omnipotence of God should be defined as "God can bring to pass everything He wills."

This is the attribute of God that generates all kinds of foolish questions, such as, "Can God sin?" or "Can God make a stone too heavy for Him to lift?" In this regard, several things need to be noted. For one thing, there are things God cannot do. He cannot sin; He cannot even be tempted (Jas. 1:13). God cannot lie (Titus 1:2; Num. 23:19; 1 Sam. 15:29; Heb. 6:18), nor can God deny Himself (2 Tim. 2:13).

It should also be remembered that God's attributes must be considered together. The problem is that each attribute is isolated and looked at independently of the others for study purposes. That can be dangerous. God is a person, not a pile of unrelated attributes. So, God would not make a stone He could not lift, even if He could, because it is not part of His purpose. To make a stone that He could not lift is stupid, and God is wise. This attribute must be considered in conjunction with the others. Omnipotence is, by definition, the ability of God to bring to pass everything He wills. That does not diminish the power of God. He is powerful and has all the power.

Humans have created some powerful forces, but compared to God's power, that's a child's strength compared to a professional weight lifter. For example, "A volcanic eruption is more powerful than an H-Bomb; an earthquake is one hundred thousand times more powerful than an Atom bomb; a hurricane lifts sixty million, or more, tons of water and generates more power every ten seconds than all the electric power used in the United States in a year! One flash of lightning would keep any home lit for thirty-five years. Hurricane Carla, three hundred and fifty miles in diameter, one of the most violent hurricanes in recorded weather history, whirled in from the Gulf of Mexico onto the coast of Texas. She had ninety times as much energy as Russia's fifty megaton bomb and pushed forty-six million tons of water before her" (*Robert G. Lee's Sourcebook of 500 Illustration*, p. 145). That's a small sample of God's mighty power.

Holiness God is holy. Moses wrote, "For I am the Lord your God. You shall, therefore, satisfy yourselves, and you shall be holy for I am holy. Neither shall you defile yourselves with any creeping thing that creeps on the earth" (Lev. 11:44).

What does holiness mean? The Hebrew word means "to set apart." God is set apart from His creatures (Isa. 57:15). God is exalted above His creatures in infinite majesty. He is transcendent. He is also set apart from sin (Lev. 11:43-45; Deut. 23:14). Just as health is more than the absence of disease, so holiness is more than absence from sin. It is moral perfection and purity.

It is clear in the Scriptures that God is holy and He wants believers to be holy. He is set apart from sin and pure. He wants believers to be set apart from sin and, like Himself, be holy. The argument that God is holy and, therefore, we should be holy is used in both the Old Testament (Lev. 11:44) and the New Testament (1 Pet. 1:16).

Righteousness God is righteous. Ezra said, "Oh Lord God of Israel, you are righteous, for we are left as a remnant as it were this day. Here we are before you in our guilt though no one can stand before you because of this" (Ezra 9:15). The righteousness of God includes the justice of God. In fact, in Hebrew and Greek, the words for "righteous" and "justice" are the same.

The basic idea of righteousness is "conformity to the law." God is righteous because He acts according to the law—not a law above Him, but a law within Him. It is the very nature of God that leads Him to do what is right. Theologians have concluded that righteousness is close to holiness. Shedd said that righteousness is a "mode of holiness." Others have said it is a manifestation of holiness. Holiness is what God is in Himself; righteousness is that character expressed in His dealings with men.

Righteousness is an attribute of God, which does what is right because it is right. It is devoid of all emotion, passion, personal preference, or caprice. It is vindicative, not vindictive.

God is right when He punishes sin (Ezra 9:15). People are guilty before God and, thus, God is righteous in punishing sin. God is also righteous when He forgives sin (1 Jn. 1:9). Christ paid for sin, so when men trust Christ and that payment is applied, God is righteous to forgive.

Loving and Gracious God is loving. The apostle John said, "He who does not love does not know God, for God is love" (1 Jn. 4:8). God is also gracious. The psalmist said, "Gracious is the Lord and righteous, yes, our God is merciful" (Ps. 116:5). God is loving, gracious, merciful, and kind. All of these characteristics speak of the goodness of God.

The biblical concept of love is that it does what is best for the other person, even when that means a sacrifice to the one loving

(Jn. 3:16). Grace means "favor." God shows favor and so do people. People do it because someone has earned it or because they want something from someone. When God grants a favor, it is not because anyone earned it or even deserved it. It is solely because He is loving, gracious, and kind. A gracious act of God was in giving His Son to die for sin (Titus 2:11).

If you wish to know the love of God, look at the nail-pierced hands of Christ. Years ago, in England, a man named William Dixon lived in Brackenthwaite. He was a widower who also lost his only son. One day, the house of one of his neighbors caught fire. The aged owner was rescued, but her orphaned grandson was trapped in the blaze. Dixon climbed an iron pipe on the side of the house and lowered the boy to safety. As a result of holding on to the pipe, his hands were severely burned. Shortly after the fire, the grandmother died. The townspeople wondered who would care for the boy.

Two volunteers appeared before the town council. One was a father who had lost his son. The other was William Dixon. When it came time for William to speak, instead of saying anything, he merely held up his scarred hand. When the vote was taken, the boy was given to him.

Faithfulness God is faithful. Paul said, "No temptation has overtaken you except such as is common to man; but God is faithful, who will not allow you to be tempted beyond what you are able but with the temptation will also make a way of escape that you may be able to bear it" (1 Cor. 10:13). God is faithful, that is, He is trustworthy and dependable. He will always fulfill His promises.

Summary: God's characteristics can be divided into His incommunicable and communicable attributes. His incommunicable attributes include sovereignty, omnipresence, and immutability. His communicable attributes include his omniscience, omnipresence, holiness, righteousness, love, graciousness, and faithfulness. More attributes could be listed.

There are problems with such a treatment of the attributes of God. For one thing, none of the attributes are incommunicable in the sense that there is no trace of them in humanity and that none of them are communicable in the sense that they are found in people as they are found in God.

The other problem with dividing God's attributes into two categories is that it does not produce a harmonious concept of God. Somehow, these two categories need to be kept together. The way to do that is to recognize that the attributes belonging to the first class qualify all those belonging to the second. For example, God is sovereign and immutable in His omniscience, omnipotence, holiness, righteousness, and graciousness.

As I have studied the Scriptures, I have been struck by the fact that all of these attributes of God are mentioned repeatedly. The Old Testament emphasizes that God is holy (Lev. 11:44) and the New Testament stresses God is love (1 Jn. 4:8). Around holiness can be grouped such attributes as truth, righteousness, and justice; clustered about love are grace, mercy, and kindness. Thus, the two major attributes of God are holiness (truth, righteousness, justice) and love (grace, mercy, kindness).

Those two basic attributes are emphasized over and over again throughout the Scripture, in the Pentateuch (Ex. 34:5-8), in the Psalms (Ps. 108:4: "For Your mercy *is* great above the heavens, and Your truth *reaches* to the clouds;" this is one example of many), in the Prophets (Micah 6:8: "He has shown you, O man, what *is* good; and what does the LORD require of you but to do justly, to love mercy, and to walk humbly with your God?"), in the Gospels (in Mt.: 23:23: Jesus said, "the weightier *matters* of the law (are) justice and mercy and faith"), and in the epistles (Eph. 4:15: "speaking the truth in love").

To be godly, believers must be righteous (Heb. 5:13) and loving (Eph. 4:15). When Paul sums up the spiritual qualities to be pursued, he mentions different attributes in these two lists, but the two characteristics that are the same in both lists are righteousness and love (1 Tim. 6:11; 2 Tim. 2:22). Righteousness without love is judgmental. Love without righteousness is sentimentality. Being God-like is being both righteous and loving. These two things are not in conflict with each other. What is right is loving and what is truly loving is right.

Knowing about God enables us to trust Him and obey Him. If you think God can make mistakes or is incapable of controlling the smallest events of life, it will not be easy to walk with Him in trusting obedience, but if you see God in a balanced biblical perspective, you will be more inclined to trust Him. You'll see He is big enough to fling stars into space and yet is concerned enough to regulate the details of life.

Knowing about God enables us to be more like Him. Repeatedly, the Scripture argues we ought to be like God. Believers should be like God in holiness (Lev. 11:44; 1 Pet. 1:6) and love (1 Jn. 4:11), and forgiveness (Eph. 4:32).

Years ago, I counseled with a lady who had a great sense of justice. She was quick to see injustice and demand justice. One day I said to her, "Your sense of justice is good. It's godlike, but God is also gracious. You need to be more like God. Keep your sense of justice. Develop graciousness."

CHAPTER 4

THE TRINITY: THE MIND-BOGGLING DOCTRINE

Many colleges and universities insist that their seniors take a battery of exams called comprehensives. These tests cover everything in the student's major. When I was a member of the Dallas Seminary pastoral ministries department, we did something similar with men about to graduate. We called it a pre-ordination exam.

Two or three faculty members would meet with a small group of students and examine one student per class during the semester. This oral exam covered their conversion, call to preach, knowledge of the Bible, theology, and the practical aspects of pastoral ministry. Imagine sitting before several faculty members, some of your classmates, and a professor asking you any question he wanted to ask about the Bible or theology.

During one of those exams, a professor asked a student, "What is the most basic doctrine of Christianity?" How would you have answered that? The Bible? The deity of Christ? Salvation by faith? The student didn't know. Of course, everyone in the room wanted to know what the professor thought. After a long pause, he said, "The Trinity."

Many would agree. In his book *The Trinity and Christian Devotion*, Charles Lowry called the doctrine of the Trinity "at once the ultimate and supreme doctrine of the Christian faith."

A professor of theology once said, "The doctrine of the Trinity ... is no doubt the one basic Christian belief when it is thought of comprehensively as to include redemption" (Kenneth Grider in *Basic Christian Doctrine*, ed. Carl Henry, pp. 39-40).

The doctrine of the Trinity is the most basic doctrine of Christianity, yet it is the most mind-bending and mind-boggling doctrine. Lewis Sperry Chafer said it is "the greatest mystery of all revealed truth." He went on to say, "The nature of God must present mysteries to the finite mind and the triune mode of existence is perhaps the supreme mystery" (Lewis Sperry Chafer, *Systematic Theology*, vol. 1, p. 273). Berkhof agrees: "The doctrine of the Trinity has always bristled with difficulties" (L. Berkhof, *Systematic Theology*, p. 82). When theologians write on this subject, they usually start by saying something like, "Neither I nor anyone else understands the Trinity."

Consequently, many have rejected the doctrine of the Trinity outright. Thomas Jefferson discounted it as "incomprehensible jargon." Matthew Arnold dismissed it as a "fairy tale."

What is this doctrine that is so difficult to understand and has caused so much difficulty? Why is it so difficult and what difference does it make?

What is the Doctrine of the Trinity?

The Scripture To understand anything concerning the doctrine of the Trinity, one must begin by looking at the simple statements of Scripture. On the one hand, the Bible dogmatically declares that there is one God (Deut. 6:4; Jas. 2:19; etc.). On the other hand, it indicates three persons in the Godhead. For example, the Great Commission instructs that believers are to be baptized in the name (note the word "name" as in the singular) of the Father, Son, and Holy Spirit (Mt. 28:19). The Scripture refers to three "persons" as God: The Father (Jn. 6:27), Jesus Christ (Jn. 1:1), and the Holy Spirit (Acts 5:3-4).

That's the problem with the doctrine of the Trinity. There is one God, yet there are three persons in the Godhead. How can that be? How can there be one yet three at the same time? Candidly, I don't know. I don't understand it either! No one does, but I do not have to understand it for it to be true, for me to appreciate it, or, for that matter, for me to use it.

I don't understand electricity. Ultimately, no one does. Some say the electrons run inside the wire. Others say the electrons run outside the wire. No one knows for sure. Yet I believe in electricity. I appreciate it, though I don't appreciate the bills when I use it.

The Doctrine What we can do is define the doctrine and illustrate it. Ryrie says that one of the best definitions is B. B. Warfield's: "There is only one God, but in the unity of the Godhead, there are three eternal and co-equal persons, the same in substance but different in subsistence" (Charles C. Ryrie, *Basic Theology*, p. 53). The point is the latter part of the definition: "The same in substance," that is, each person in the Godhead is deity and "distinct in subsistence," meaning there are three separate persons. So, there is one, yet there are three. That's the part that is impossible to understand!

To illustrate the Trinity, theologians and teachers have pointed to the egg. One egg has three parts: the shell, the white, and the yolk. Likewise, there is one God who exists in three persons. The problem with that illustration is that the three parts are made up of three different substances. In the Trinity, the three parts are the same substance. Nevertheless, the egg illustrates three parts of a unit.

Some have suggested that H_2O is a better illustration. H_2O can exist as steam, water, and ice. That illustrates that the Trinity is the same in substance, but there is something wrong with that illustration too. Besides the fact that the parts are not persons, there are three parts without the unity of being one.

It has been suggested, however, that when a small amount of water is placed in a plastic tube and a vacuum is pulled on the tube, at a point, for a split second, there will be steam in one end of the tube, water in the middle and ice at the other end at the same time in one place. If such an experiment is possible, it illustrates the Trinity in that there are three parts of the same substance. That illustration has a problem in that the parts are not persons. Oh well, no one understands the Trinity anyway.

Augustine's explanation of the Trinity is summarized in seven statements: 1) the Father is God, 2) the Son is God, 3) the Holy Spirit is God, 4) the Father is not the Son, 5) the Son is not the Holy Spirit, 6) the Holy Spirit is not the Father, 7) There is only one God.

As he was walking on the shore, Augustine was meditating on the great perplexity of the doctrine of the Trinity when he observed a little boy with a seashell running to the water, filling his shell, and pouring it into a hole that he had made in the sand. "What are you doing, little man?" asked Augustine, "Oh," replied the boy, "I am trying to put the ocean in this hole." Augustine thought to himself, "That is what I am trying to do. I am standing on the shore of time trying to get into these little finite-minded things that are infinite." John Wesley said, "Bring me a worm that can comprehend a man and I'll show you a man that can comprehend God."

What the Doctrine of the Trinity is Not

Maybe the best that can be done is to explain what the Bible does not mean by the doctrine of the Trinity.

Modalism On the surface, these facts seem to contradict each other. So, the temptation is to take one truth and exclude the other. Some teach, for example, that God is one and, therefore, not three persons. In this view, called modalism, there is one God who, before the birth of Christ, existed in heaven as God the Father. At the birth of Christ, He became the Son. When the Son returned to heaven, He returned as the Holy Spirit. According to this view, the three persons in the Godhead are merely three successive manifestations of the one God.

A simple illustration of this heresy is a three-act play. In Act 1, a man emerges on the stage dressed in a long gray beard and hobbling on a cane, like Father Time. In Act 2, as the curtain goes up, the same man is on center stage; only this time, he is dressed in the attire of a young man. In Act 3, the same person is dressed like a ghost.

Modalism is not the biblical doctrine of the Trinity; it is heresy. There is not one divine person manifesting Himself in three different ways. That is obvious from the baptism of Christ, where as soon as Christ came up from the water, the Holy Spirit descended on Him and a voice from heaven said, "This is my beloved Son, in whom I am well pleased" (Mt. 3:17). In this incident, all three members of the Trinity are present at the same time, indicating that the Trinity is not one person manifesting Himself in three different ways at different times.

Tri-theism The other error is to go to the other extreme. Some teach that there are three persons, all called God. They think of

God the same way they think of Peter, James, and John, as three separate individuals only loosely related to each other. This is called tri-theism.

The Persons of the Trinity are distinct but not separate. Chafer says, "The Trinity is composed of three united Persons without separate existence—so completely united as to form one God" (Lewis Sherry Chafer, *Systematic Theology*, vol. 1, p. 276).

To illustrate the threeness and yet oneness, some have referred to sunshine. Sunshine is composed of three elements: heat rays, which can be felt but not seen; light rays, which can be seen but not felt; and chemical rays, which cannot be seen or felt but have effects. Altogether, they make up light, three rays, yet one light. Without any of them, there would be no light. Likewise, one God exists in three distinct but not separate persons.

Perhaps a simple illustration of the Trinity is a single equilateral triangle that consists of three equal angles and three equal lines.

Berkhof has concluded, "The many efforts that were made to explain the mystery were speculative rather than theological. They inevitably result in the development of tri-theism or modalistic concepts of God, in the denial of either the unity of the Divine Essence or the reality of the personal distinctions within the essence" (L. Berkhof, *Systematic Theology*, p. 89).

Why Believe in the Trinity?

If there is so much misunderstanding concerning this doctrine, why do Christians insist on it? If it is impossible to understand it, why believe it? Furthermore, it has hindered some from becoming Christians. W. A. Rice wrote in *The Crusaders in the Twentieth Century*, "Nothing could be easier than to win proselytes among Hindus and Muslims if only the doctrine of the Trinity were given up" (Rice, cited by Chafer in his *Systematic Theology*, vol. 1, p. 287).

Not Creeds Jehovah's Witnesses contend that the only reason anyone believes in the Trinity is because of early councils and creeds. According to them, the doctrine of the Trinity is not in the Bible at all. Tertullian, who lived about AD 200, was the first person to use the word Trinity. The Council of Nicea was the first official formulation of the doctrine, and that was in AD 325. So, they say, it is the doctrine of man and not the doctrine of God. Granted, the word Trinity is not in the Bible, but the idea is. Admittedly, the Council of Nicea was the first official formulation of the doctrine in church history, but that was because a great discussion and debate arose over the relationship between Jesus Christ and the Holy Spirit to God. Arius taught that Christ was a created being. Athanasius taught that Christ was not created but was God. A council was called to settle the issue, and the Nicene Creed was written. That was the first formulation in church history of the doctrine of the Trinity, but the idea was in the Bible long before that.

New Testament The New Testament teaches the doctrine of the Trinity. As was stated earlier, each member of the Trinity was recognized as God. The baptism of Christ reveals the Trinity (Mt. 3:16, 17). The statements of the Lord Himself record the fact that he spoke of the Trinity (Mt. 28:19; Jn. 14:16). Even the benediction of Paul points to the Trinity. At the conclusion of 2 Corinthians, he said, "The grace of the Lord Jesus Christ and the love of God and the communion of the Holy Spirit will be with you all. Amen" (2 Cor. 13:14). He did not say, "The grace of Jesus Christ, the love of Brother Brown, and the communion of Sister Smith." He put Jesus Christ and the Holy Spirit on the same par as God.

The doctrine of the Trinity is not an isolated, obscure doctrine in the back room of the New Testament. It is in every room. Consider: Mt. 3:16, 17; 28:19; Jn. 14:16, 26; 16:13-16; 1 Cor. 12:4-6; 2 Cor. 13:14; Eph. 1:13-14; 4:4-6; Col. 1:3-8; 1 Pet. 1:2; 1 Jn. 4:2; Jude 20-21, and so forth!

Old Testament Is the doctrine of the Trinity revealed in the Old Testament? The Jews, of course, would say, "Not at all!" Some Protestant preachers claim that the Old Testament completely reveals the Trinity. Both views are mistaken. The progressive views of God's revelation must not be disregarded. While the doctrine of the Trinity is not fully revealed in the Old Testament, it is intimated and implied.

The doctrine of the Trinity is implied in the Old Testament by using the plural word for God. In English, words are singular or plural, but in Hebrew, a word can be singular, dual, or plural. Therefore, a plural is more than two. The Hebrew word for God, "Elohim," is not in the singular or dual but in the plural. Thus, the very word for God demands three (or more). The opening verse of Genesis says, "In the beginning, God (*Elohim*, a plural word) created (a singular verb) the heavens (a dual word; two heavens were created, the third heaven is eternal) and earth (a singular word)" (Gen. 1:1).

The doctrine of the Trinity is also seen in the Old Testament by using the personal pronoun. In Genesis 1:26, God said, "Let us make man in Our image." It is futile to argue that God referred to angels because verse 27 says, "So God created man in His own image. In the image of God, He created them."

The term "the Spirit of God" also argues for the Trinity. In the Old Testament, there is a difference between the Lord and His Spirit (Gen. 1:2; Isa. 48:16). The Spirit of God is not just some force or influence, for He is called "Counselor" in Isaiah 40:13.

Still, another indication of the Trinity in the Old Testament is the appearance of the Angel of the Lord (Gen. 16:7; etc.). From the title, it might appear that He is an angel. However, a close examination of the passages where He appears indicates that He is God (Gen. 16:13). In Genesis 16, the Angel of the Lord is identified with God. In other passages, He is distinct from Him (Judges 13:16).

There are other indications of the Trinity in the Old Testament, some subtle and some not so subtle (Isa. 48:16). In Isaiah 6:3, the Seraphim cry, "Holy, Holy, Holy." In the same passage, the Lord Himself asked, "Who will go for us?" (Isa. 6:8). Granted, these are not "proofs." They are only indications, but after the floodlight of the New Testament revelation, believers begin to see and understand the lesser lights of the Old Testament on this doctrine.

I once asked a theology professor why the doctrine of the Trinity was not revealed in the Old Testament. He responded, "For the same reason, it is not revealed in the New Testament." For a moment, I was a bit taken aback. He then went on to say, "It is assumed. It is like the Atlantic Ocean. No sign says this ocean is salty, but everywhere you dip your finger to taste, you know it's salty. Likewise, there is no 'sign' in the Bible saying, 'God is a Trinity,' but everywhere you look, you bump into that truth."

Summary: Christians believe in the doctrine of the Trinity, namely, that there is one God, but in the unity of the Godhead, there are three eternal and coequal Persons, the same in substance but different in subsistence, because the Bible reveals it.

Although the concept is complex, and Christians admit they do not comprehend threeness and oneness (Trinity in unity; unity in Trinity), they are convinced of it because the Bible teaches it. Neither basic arithmetic nor higher math will suffice. Christians propagate the doctrine of the Trinity not because they have figured it out by human reason but because they found it in Divine revelation.

One theologian put it like this: "We do not hold the doctrine of the Trinity because it is self-evident or logically cogent. We hold it because God has revealed that this is what He is like. As someone has said of this doctrine: try to explain it and you'll lose your mind. But try to deny it and you'll lose your soul" (Lewis Sherry Chafer, *Systematic Theology*, vol. 1, p. 273).

Should it surprise anyone that no one understands the nature of God? After all, does anyone understand the nature of human beings? Psychiatrists and psychologists try, but there are almost as many theories to explain people as people studying people. How many men have said to their wives, "I'll never understand you!?" If humans cannot understand humans, how can anyone expect humans to understand God?

It has been suggested that the universe's very structure reflects the Trinity. The universe consists of matter, space, and time. Matter is energy, motion, and phenomena. Space is height, length, and breadth. Time is past, present, and future (Nathan R. Wood, *The Trinity in the University*, Grand Rapids: Kregel Publications, 1978).

Assuming the truth of the Trinity, what is the application of that doctrine to daily life? If the Trinity is true, the Trinity is the ultimate reality. The Trinity existed before people or even the universe was created, so how do we relate the eternal, ultimate reality of the Trinity to practical everyday life in time?

The doctrine of the eternal Trinity teaches that ultimate reality consists of relationships. When there was no universe as we know it, the members of the Trinity related to each other. No being has ever lived alone in isolation. The doctrine of the Trinity teaches us to value relationships and develop relationships. You will value relationships if you wish to live your life based on eternal values. One author has put it like this: "There is a richness in this dogma. It means that God is no bare nomad but an eternal fellowship. It is exciting to realize that God did not exist in solitary aloneness from all eternity, prior to the creation of the world and man, but in a blessed communion" (Ryrie, *Basic Christian Doctrine*, p. 40).

A friend wrote a paper for a seminary class on small groups. When he wanted to prove from the Bible that Christians ought to meet in small groups, he began with the doctrine of the Trinity.

The doctrine of the eternal Trinity indicates that ultimate reality consists of love. God is love (1 Jn. 4:8). If you wish to live your life based on eternal values, you will live a loving life. "God so loved the world that He gave His only begotten Son" (Jn. 3:16). A loving life gives of oneself to benefit and bless others.

The doctrine of the eternal Trinity implies that ultimate reality consists of unity. Members of the Trinity live in unity and harmony.

The doctrine of the eternal truth of the Trinity involves that ultimate reality consists of submission. The Trinity consists of God the Father, God the Son, and God the Holy Spirit. There has been a debate in church history over whether or not God the Son was the eternal Son or became the Son at His incarnation. In my opinion, the Bible teaches that Jesus Christ was the eternal Son of God, meaning that He was the Son in eternity past. His eternal Sonship does not mean anything less than a deity or eternally equal to God the Father. It does mean that He was submissive to the Father. If that is true, submission is part of eternal, ultimate reality. If you wish to base your life on eternal values, you will have to practice submission in your daily life. Paul argues that the Head of Christ is God, the Head of man is Christ and the head of the woman is man (1 Cor. 11:3). In other words, He takes the eternal truth of the nature of the Godhead and directly applies it to the loving, submissive relationship between people and God and between a husband and a wife.

In seminary, I heard Dr. Charles Ryrie lecture on the Trinity. He said in passing, "Imagine what fellowship among the members of the Trinity must be like." I heard him say that many years ago, but I've often thought about it. I commend the exercise to you. Contemplate the Trinity. If we thought about the Trinity more and desired more to be like the Trinity, we would base our lives on eternal values and consequently live a more loving, submissive lifestyle.

CHAPTER 5

WHAT KIND OF FATHER IS GOD THE FATHER?

It sounds so simple: "Our Father in heaven." What could be difficult about that? Yet, for many today, it is often complex, complicated, and confusing.

When, for example, you say, "God is Father," what do you mean? Of whom is He the Father? Some believe in the universal fatherhood of God. Others would say it is not enough just to be born to be God's children. You must also be reborn. If that is the case, not all, only some, are God's children.

Or consider the psychological problem with the doctrine of the fatherhood of God. We form our image of a father from our human father, so when someone says God is Father, we tend to pour our concept of a father, derived from our experience with our earthly father, into that.

Some men are loving fathers who spend time, money, and energy on their children. They pray for their children, praise them when they are good, and punish them when they are bad. They hug them and, perhaps most importantly, hug their mother in front of them. Children reared by such a father have warm feelings and positive perceptions of fatherhood.

Not all children have had a father like that. Some have had no father at all, either because of death, divorce, or desertion. Their image of a father comes from who knows where: a movie, a TV program, a novel, or a father down the street. In that case, father could mean anything. He could be a good father, a bad example, or the devil incarnate.

Worse yet, some have had a father who was there, but the child wished a thousand times he were dead or that he had deserted the family. When he was at home, he was self-centered, silent, sarcastic, and perhaps even intimidating. When speaking to the children, he was negative or neutral, rarely offering positive feedback. When he punished, which was often, it was brutal. Imagine the one great memory of a father is the brutal beatings he gave, so when someone says "father" to a child reared in that kind of home, he gets nervous.

When God is called Father, who is He the Father of, and what kind of Father is He? What does He do as Father?

God is the Father of Four

An examination of how the concept of father is applied to God in the Scripture reveals that He is Father in four different senses: 1) of Jesus Christ, 2) of creation, 3) of Israel, and 4) of believers.

Jesus Christ God is the Father of Jesus Christ. John writes, "No one has seen God at any time. The only begotten Son, who is in the bosom of the Father, He has declared Him" (Jn. 1:18). Paul says, "For this reason, I bow my knees to the Father of our Lord Jesus Christ" (Eph. 3:14). At Christ's baptism, God spoke from heaven and said, "This is My beloved Son" (Mt. 3:17). Jesus is repeatedly called the Son of God. When He prayed, He said, "Father" (Jn. 17:15).

To say that God is the Father of Christ sounds like God lived a long time and had a Son named Jesus. If that's true, there was a time when Christ did not exist, making Him a created being and not God. Yet the Bible frequently refers to Jesus as possessing the attributes and works of God. So, in what sense is God the Father, the Father of Jesus Christ?

The answer is God is an eternal Father (Isa. 9:6) and to be an eternal Father, He must have an eternal Son. The term "Son" does not always refer to a son by generation. It may refer to a son in another relationship. For example, a father who has adopted a son has a son not by generation but by adoption. So, the father-son relationship is not always by birth.

Isaiah 9:6 says, "For unto us a Child is born, unto us a Son is given." Notice carefully that the *Child* is born. The *Son* is not born; He is given. The Babe in Bethlehem was born, but the life was the eternal Son. The Babe had a beginning; the Son had no beginning. He always existed from eternity with the Father, so Christ is the Son, not by generation, but by an eternal relationship.

This does not mean that Jesus Christ became the Son at His birth or at some later time. Some have said that is the case, but many have rejected that as orthodox theology. Remember, God is an eternal Father (Isa. 9:6). God the Father has always been the Father of Jesus Christ.

The creeds have expressed this truth. The words of the Nicene Creed are: "The only begotten Son of God, begotten of the Father before all worlds, God of Gods, Light of Light, very God of very God, begotten but not made, being in one substance with the Father." The Athanasian Creed puts it like this: "The Son is from the Father alone; neither made, nor created, but begotten ... generated from eternity from the substance of the Father."

In his *Systematic Theology*, Chafer observed, "It is probable that the terms *Father* and *Son* as applied to the first and second persons in the Godhead are somewhat anthropomorphic. That sublime and eternal relationship that existed between the two Persons is best expressed in human understanding in terms of *Father* and *Son*, but wholly without implication that the two Persons on the divine side are not equal in every particular" (Chafer, vol. I, p. 239).

Creation God is not only the Father of Jesus Christ, He is also said to be the Father of all creation. First Corinthians 8:6 says He is the Father "of whom are all things." In the Greek text, "of" means "out of." In other words, God is the source of the entire universe. He is the creator; all things proceed from Him. In the context of 1 Corinthians 8, Paul is making the point that nothing created by God, in this case, meat offered to idols, can defile believers.

This does not mean that all three Persons of the Trinity did not participate in creation. It just means that God the Father did, as did the others. God's involvement in creation means that He created all things. James 1:17 refers to light, including heavenly bodies like the sun, moon, and stars. God also created angels (Job 1:6; 2:1; 38:7) and all men (Mal. 2:10; Acts 17:29).

The Bible, then, teaches the universal Fatherhood of God! God is the Creator of all creation and all creatures. All things and all living creatures owe their origin to Him. In this sense only, is it proper to refer to the universal Fatherhood of God. This does not justify, however, the misuse of the doctrine by liberal theologians who use it to teach universal salvation or that God is every man's Father in the spiritual sense of the term. It is one thing to be God's creation and another to be His child (Jn. 1:10-12).

I once built a snowman. In a sense, I was its creator, but I was not its father. On the other hand, I am the father of three children.

Israel God is also the Father of Israel (Ex. 4:22), meaning more than just their Creator. In Exodus 4, Israel was God's Son, and by implication, Egypt was not. This is less than saying that they were all regenerated. Not all Israelites had spiritual life (Rom. 2:28-29). At any rate, somewhere between creation and regeneration, God had an intimate relationship with Israel. He chose to express this by the figure of Father and Son.

By contrast, God is not the Father of the United States of America. True, He blesses any nation that honors Him and insists on righteousness. When a nation turns from Him and His righteousness, punishment follows. He did that even with Israel. The difference is that He will work again with Israel, whereas with other nations, He is not obligated to do so.

Christians God is the Father of all who trust Jesus Christ. John says, "But as many as received Him, to them He gave the right to become children of God, to those who believe in His name" (Jn. 1:12). Believers are born into God's family (Jn. 1:13). All humans are God's creatures; only those who trust Christ are God's children. There is a sense in which all creatures have God as their Father. Believers have God as their Father in the full sense of the term—by birth. Those who trust Christ are children of God through regeneration and adoption (Gal. 4:5). Thus, a person is either of his father, the Devil (Jn. 8:44), or his Father—God.

There is more to being a child of God. It includes being a partaker of the divine nature (2 Pet. 1:4) and being an heir of God (Rom. 8:16-17).

Because we are sons, we cry, "Abba! Father!" (Gal. 4:6). Everyone prays to God when they get into serious trouble. Believers do it, too, but it's different. They cry, "Father." Unbelievers may pray and even hope against hope, but they never know for sure.

Believers know that they know God and are assured that He hears and cares.

God is a Loving Father

What kind of Father is God, especially to believers? His very nature is love (1 Jn. 4:8). The proof of His love is that He gave His Son to die for sin (Rom. 5:8). God's love towards His children is described in some depth toward the end of Romans 8. He *knew* each believer before He was born (Rom. 8:29; "whom" not "what"). He *chose* every believer before He was born (Rom. 8:29). He then *called* each one (Rom. 8:30), *justified* each one (Rom. 8:30), and will ultimately *glorify* each one (Rom. 8:30).

A teenager once said, "My father does not love me. He got stuck with me. He would never have chosen me to be his daughter if he had known me. He doesn't even like me." God is not like that. He knew each of His children before they were born and chose each. Then He made each individual His child by birth and, on top of that, He adopted each one. God loves His children.

Provides Exactly what kind of loving Father is God? Among other things, He provides for them physically (Mt. 6:25, 26, 28-30). I've experienced the Lord doing this for me repeatedly. For example, when I first graduated from seminary and started traveling as an itinerant evangelist, I was invited to small churches. The size of the check was like the size of the church. In those days, we managed to eat but didn't have much money beyond that.

I remember being in a small rural church and counseling with a lady. She had been hospitalized twice in the two previous years. The doctor had said there was nothing physically wrong with her. Her problems were spiritual, not physical. By the grace of God,

I was able to help. At the end of the week, her husband came to me and said, "Young man, I have a feeling you have saved me a great deal of money on hospital and doctor bills. Thanks." He then slipped enough money into my palm for me to buy a much-needed suit. God clothes the lilies of the field, and He clothes His children.

God provides physically and spiritually (Eph. 1:3; Col. 2:10). God provides everything believers need to live a godly life. Many believers don't live as if they own all spiritual blessings because they don't utilize what they have, yet God has provided it. When my son was a preschooler, he used a one-gallon can for a chair. His grandmother gave him a beautiful children's rocker, but he sat on the can instead of the chair! God has provided us with a comfortable rocker, and we sit on rocks.

Protects As a loving Father, God provides for His children and protects them (Jude 24; Jn. 17:15). When we think of protection, we immediately think of physical danger. God indeed protects His children physically, but He also protects them spiritually. He protects them from Satan and sin.

Shepherds in Palestine drive their sheep into sheepfolds in the evening. These folds have an enclosed wall with one opening, but that opening has no gate or door. The shepherd himself is the door. He lies across the doorway when the sheep are in for the night. No sheep can get out except over his body and no wolf or thief can get in except over him. In a similar fashion, God protects His own.

Punishes As a loving Father, God also punishes His children (Heb. 12:5-7). Love and punishment are two concepts that are not generally put together, but they should be (Prov. 13:24). Because God loves, He chastens.

The purpose, though, is not punishment as such. The intent is to draw the believer closer to Him, rather than farther away. God may rock a believer's boat, especially if it will bring the believer closer to Him.

A little boy's toy boat floated beyond his reach. In his distress, he appealed to a bigger boy for help. Saying nothing, the older boy picked up stones and began throwing them toward the boat. The little boy was even more upset, thinking the one to whom he had turned for help was about to destroy his prized possession. Shortly, however, he noticed that instead of hitting the boat, each stone landed beyond it, making a small ripple that moved the vessel closer to the shore. Every throw of the stone was planned, and at last, the boy's treasured boat was brought back to the harbor into the waiting hands of its owner. Likewise, God causes ripples in our lives to draw us closer to Him.

Summary: God is the Father of Christ, of creation, and of Israel, as well as believers. As a loving Father, He provides, protects, and punishes.

Where do you get your concept of God? From your human father? If you do, you may think of Him as a policeman who enforces the law or as a judge who punishes lawbreakers. Or do you get your concept of God from your response to Him? If that is the case, you may feel He loves you, but that He loves you like your love for Him, which is partial, moody, and even selfish. Our concept of God should come from the Scripture; if it does, we will see Him as a loving Father. His love for us is unselfish and never moody.

A seriously ill saint confided in a friend about his lack of love for the Lord. His friend responded by saying, "When I go home,

I expect to take my baby on my knee, look into her eyes, listen to her charming conversation and, tired as I am, her presence will rest me for I love that child with indescribable tenderness, but she loves me little. If my heart were breaking, it would not disturb her sleep. If my body were wracked with pain, it would not interrupt her play. If I were dead, she would forget me in a few days. Besides this, she has never brought me a penny, but is a constant expense to me. I am not rich, but there is not enough money in the world to buy my daughter. How is it? Does she love me, or do I love her? Do I withhold my love until I know she loves me? Am I waiting for her to do something worthy of my love before I extend it?"

You see, it is not the believer's love for God but God's love for His children that should first occupy the minds of believers. As it does, believers will end up loving God because God first loved them.

CHAPTER 6

THE WORLD'S MOST INTRIGUING PERSON

Jesus Christ is the world's most intriguing person. On July 11, 1926, at a youth meeting at the Shrine Auditorium in Los Angeles, James Allan Frances, the Pastor of the First Baptist Church of Los Angeles, delivered a sermon that has become well known as "One Solitary Life." It reads as follows:

> Here is a young man who was born in an obscure village, the child of a peasant woman. He grew up in another village. He worked in a carpenter shop until He was thirty, and then for three years, He was an itinerant preacher. He never wrote a book. He never held an office. He never owned a home. He never had a family. He never went to college. He never put His foot inside a big city. He never traveled 200 miles from the place where He was born. He never did one of the things that usually accompany greatness. He had no credentials but Himself.
>
> While He was still a young man, the tide of public opinion turned against Him. His friends ran away. He was turned over to His enemies. He went through the mockery of a trial. He was nailed to the cross between two thieves. While He was dying,

His executioners gambled for the only piece of property He had on earth, and that was His coat. When He was dead, He was laid in a borrowed grave through the pity of a friend.

Nineteen centuries have come and gone, and today He is the central figure of the human race and the leader of the column of progress. I am far within the mark when I say that all the armies that ever marched, and all the navies that ever sailed, and all the parliaments that ever sat, and all the kings that ever reigned, put together, have not affected the life of man upon this earth as has that One Solitary Life.

That's only the beginning. Much more could be said about Him and everything about Him is intriguing. Trying to cover all the aspects of Christ is like trying to cover all of the books in the Huntington Library. The Bible lists over 250 names for Christ. Here are just a few:

> The Bible calls Him Advocate, Adam, Apostle, and Ancient of Days.
> The Bible calls Him Bread, Bridegroom, Begotten of the Father, Brightness of the Father's Image.
> The Bible calls Him Covenant, Counselor, Chief Cornerstone, Christ.
> The Bible calls Him Deliverer, Desire of All Nations, Door.
> The Bible calls Him Everlasting Father, Eternal One.

The Bible calls Him Forerunner, Firstfruits of them that slept, Faithful Witness, Friend of the Church.
The Bible calls Him Gift of God, Governor, Guide, and God.
The Bible calls Him Head of the Church, Horn of Salvation, Hearer of All Things.
The Bible calls Him Immanuel, Invincible, Inheritance, and I Am.
The Bible calls Him Jesus, Just One.
The Bible calls Him King of Kings.
The Bible calls Him Lord of Lords, and Lamb, and Love, and Light, and Life.
The Bible calls Him Messenger, Messiah.
The Bible calls Him Nazarene.
The Bible calls Him the Only Savior, Omnipotent, Omniscient.
The Bible calls Him Priest, and Prince of Peace, and Potentate, and Passover.
The Bible calls Him Refuge, Resurrection, Rose of Sharon, Redeemer, Root of David, Ransom, Rest.
The Bible calls Him Stone, Son of God, Servant, Seed of Woman, Savior.
The Bible calls Him Teacher, Tabernacle, Tree of Life, Truth.
The Bible calls Him Wonderful, Witness, the Word, the Wisdom of God.

More can be said about Christ than any book or set of books could contain (Jn. 21:25). The biblical teaching concerning Christ, however, is usually succinctly summarized under two headings—His Person and His Work.

His Person

Jesus Christ is God The Bible teaches that Jesus Christ is God. That shocks some, probably because they are used to referring to Him as the Son of God, which is perfectly proper. Nonetheless, the Bible teaches that Jesus Christ is God by direct and indirect statements.

Jesus Christ is called Immanuel, which means "God with us" (Isa. 7:14; Mt. 1:18-25). What could be clearer!

He is also called the Mighty God (Isa. 9:6-7). Jehovah's Witnesses object that there is a difference between Jesus being the Mighty God (they consider Him *a* God) and Jehovah, who is the Almighty God. However, the Bible teaches that God is both mighty and almighty (Jer. 32:17-18).

John 1:1 says, "The Word was God," while verse 14 says, "The Word became flesh." Again, the Jehovah's Witnesses object, saying there is no article in the Greek text of John 1:1. Therefore, it should be translated "The Word was *a* God." They fail to recognize that in Koine Greek, the absence of an article emphasizes quality. In the case of John 1:1, the lack of the article indicates that the Word was deity!

Philippians 2:6 is another direct statement of Christ's deity. It says He was "in the form of God." The Greek word translated as "form" refers to His essential attributes.

Colossians 1:15 declares Him to be "the image of the invisible God." The Greek word translated as "image" does not mean that He resembles God, but rather that He is a representation or copy of God. It was used in the ancient world as a dye, producing an exact likeness.

Those who deny the deity of Christ point out that in this verse, He is also called the firstborn of all creation, claiming that He is a created being and not the eternal God, but "firstborn" is a figure of speech that means "first in rank," not "first in time" (Ps. 89:27). Besides, the figure in Colossians 1:15 is not claiming that Jesus was created, because the next verse says that He created all things. He could not create all things if He were created.

First Timothy 3:16 proclaims, "<u>God</u> was manifested in the flesh." Some Greek texts read, "<u>He</u> was manifested in the flesh," but the majority of manuscripts contain the reading found in the King James and New King James Versions.

Titus 2:13 should be translated "Looking for the blessed hope and glorious appearing of our great God, even Savior, Jesus Christ."

If the Bible is the Word of God, Jesus is the Son of God, that is, God the Son.

There are also indirect indications in the Bible of Christ's deity. Consider His titles. He is called the Son of God (Jn. 5:18, 25). He is also referred to as the Lord (Acts 16:31). William Evans quotes Wood as saying, "The Ptolemys and the Roman Emperors would allow the name to be applied to them only when they permitted themselves to be deified. The archeological discoveries at Oxyrhynchus put this fact beyond a doubt. So, when the New Testament writers speak of Jesus as Lord, there can be no question as to what they mean" (Evans, *Great Doctrines of the Bible*, p. 60).

Isaiah 41:4 refers to Jehovah as the First and the Last, but John says that this refers to Jesus Christ (Rev. 22:12-13, 20). Something similar could be said about the title Alpha and Omega (Rev. 1:8; 12:13, 20).

Not only the appellations but also the attributes attributed to Christ indicate His deity. The New Testament claims He is omnipotent (Mt. 28:18), omniscient (Jn. 2:24, 16:30), omnipresent (Mt. 28:20), and immutable (Heb. 13:8). As Evans said, "All nature, which like a garment He throws around Him, is subject to change and decay. Jesus Christ is the same always; He never changes" (Evans, *Great Doctrines of the Bible*, p. 62).

Christ's activities also portray His deity. He created the world (Jn. 1:3) and He forgives sin (Lk. 7:48). He was worshiped (Mt. 2:11). When mere mortals were worshiped in the New Testament, they rebuked the worshipers (Acts 10:25, 26), but when Christ was worshiped, He did not correct the worshipers (Jn. 20:28). Either Jesus Christ was God or an imposter.

Robert Browning is reported to have said, "When Charles Lamb and some of his friends were discussing how they would feel if the greatest of the dead were to appear suddenly in flesh and blood, that Lamb said, 'If Shakespeare entered, we should all rise. If Christ appeared, we must kneel.'"

Jesus was a man. Jesus Christ was God, but He became a man. He was born of a woman (Mt. 1:18; Gal. 4:4), and grew as a child (Lk. 2:40, 52). He must have had a human appearance because He was recognized as a Jew by features and speech (Jn. 4:9). Furthermore, He experienced human needs, such as hunger (Mt. 4:2), thirst (Jn. 19:28), sleep (Mt. 8:24), being weary (Jn. 4:6), and even weeping (Jn. 11). No wonder He was called the Son of Man at least eighty times in the Gospel of Luke alone and referred to as the Man, Christ Jesus, in 1 Timothy 2:5. By the way, His head had no halo.

In short, Jesus is God and Jesus is Man. He is called the Son of God and the Son of Man (Mt. 26:63, 64). There is none, no one, quite like the God/Man, Jesus Christ.

His Work

While many things Christ did on earth could be classified as "His work," the two main things He did were to die and rise from the dead.

Jesus died. It is said that the death of Christ is mentioned 175 times in the New Testament, one out of every forty-four verses. When you add to these figures the typical and symbolic teaching of the Old Testament, you understand the important place this doctrine occupies in the sacred Scriptures (Evans, *Great Doctrines in the Bible*, p. 70).

Other great people said, in essence, "Let me live and I will accomplish great things." Jesus said, "I came so that I could die." Others are valued for their lives, but Jesus is valued for His death.

The theological implications of Jesus Christ's death have occupied the minds of the greatest theologians for centuries. To summarize the profound spiritual truth in one short, simple sentence: Jesus Christ became our substitute to pay for sin, so that people could have a relationship with God. This fantastic concept encompasses four key aspects: Jesus, God, sin, and people. Doctrinally, those four aspects are referred to as substitution, propitiation, redemption, and reconciliation.

Jesus died as a substitute (Isa. 53:6). People have sinned and the penalty is death, but the Lord laid on Jesus the iniquity of us all. Jesus Christ became our substitute, dying in our place to pay for our sins.

Jesus died to be a propitiation for our sin (1 Jn. 2:2). Propitiation means satisfaction. Being just, God demands that death be the payment for sin. When Jesus died, He satisfied the justice and wrath of God. The payment was made by Jesus. As a father paid for his teenage son's speeding ticket and his payment satisfied the just demand of the law, so Jesus paid for our sins and satisfied the just demand of God.

The doctrine of propitiation is: Because Jesus died as a substitute for people's sin, God's justice are satisfied, and therefore people can be saved (1 Jn. 2:2).

Jesus died to redeem us (Titus 2:14). Redemption means to buy back and set free. Jesus said, "Whosoever commits sin is the slave of sin" (Jn. 8:34). By His death, Jesus paid for sin and provided for us to be free from sin that has enslaved us. Just as in the first century, a wealthy man could buy a slave and then set him free, so Jesus paid for sin so He could set sinners free.

The doctrine of redemption holds that because Jesus died as a substitute for people's sins, sin has now been atoned for, allowing people to be set free from their sins (Titus 2:14).

Jesus died to reconcile us to God (Rom. 5:10). We were alienated and separated from God because of our sin. The death of Jesus removed the enmity, allowing God and sinners to be reconciled. Those who were once enemies can now be friends.

The doctrine of reconciliation is that because Jesus died as a substitute for people's sin, the state of alienation from God is changed so that people can now be saved (Rom. 5:10).

Substitution is Jesus-ward; propitiation is God-ward. Redemption is sin-ward; reconciliation is people-ward. Jesus died as a substitute. God is satisfied. Sin is paid for. People are reconciled. To put it all very simply, Jesus died in our place to pay for our sins so we can have a relationship with God.

Christ Rose. After three days, He arose! His resurrection is as important as His death. It is mentioned more than 100 times in the New Testament, but more importantly, Paul states that if Jesus did not rise from the dead, then Christianity is of no account. We are still in our sin and are the most miserable of all people (1 Cor. 15:13-19).

Christianity is the only religion that bases its claim on the resurrection of its founder. All other religions say, "Come visit the tomb of our founder." Christianity says, "Our tomb is empty."

What did the resurrection of Christ accomplish? Obviously, for Him, it meant He was alive again, but what did it accomplish for others if it is so valid to Christianity? Among other things, it provides pardon and power.

The resurrection of Jesus is the assurance of our pardon (Rom. 4:25). As long as He was in the grave, we had no way of knowing that His death was acceptable to God. After all, anyone could step up and say, "I'm going to die for sin!" and then die. How would we know if that was acceptable? In the case of Jesus Christ, we know because He rose. His resurrection assures us that God accepts His death as the payment for sin.

In the Old Testament, the high priest entered the Holiest of Holies only once a year. If God accepted his offering for the nation's sins, he walked out; but if something went wrong, the high priest would not come out. In fact, tradition says they tied a rope around his foot so they could drag his body out if he were killed.

Imagine the Jews waiting outside the Tabernacle for the high priest to come out! The atmosphere was undoubtedly charged with soberness, silence, and suspense. Think of the joy and jubilation when the high priest finally strolled out. To the best of our knowledge, he always did. By his presence, they knew that his sacrifice had been accepted. Likewise, when Christ emerged from the tomb, it was the sign and signal that His sacrifice had been accepted.

The resurrection of Christ also ensures our power (Eph. 1:19-22; Phil. 3:10). There seems to be two standards by which God's power is gauged. In the Old Testament, when God wanted His people to understand the extent of His power, He pointed to His deliverance of Israel from Egypt (Micah 7:15). In the New Testament, the measure of God's power is the resurrection of Jesus (Ephesians 1:19-22; 3:20).

The death and resurrection of Jesus Christ are essential to Christianity. We need two wings, like a plane, and two tracks, like a train.

Summary: Jesus Christ is the God/Man who died for the sins of the world and bodily rose from the dead (Jn. 1:1, 14; 1 Cor. 15:3-4).

No doubt, Jesus Christ is the world's most intriguing person. He is God and yet a Man. He died and yet lives. And that is only the beginning! Much, much more could be said about this fascinating person. Someone has said it like this:

> Christ's birth was not only contrary to the usual laws of life, but the power of death could not hold Him. He had no cornfields or fisheries, but He

could spread a table of 5,000 and have bread and fish to spare. He walked upon the waters of the Sea of Galilee and they supported Him. For just three years, He preached His Gospel. When He died, few men mourned, but a black crepe was hung over the sun. Though men trembled not for their sins, the earth beneath them shook under the load. All nature honored Him. Sinners alone rejected Him. Corruption could not gain a hold on his body. The soil that had been reddened with His blood could not continue to claim His dust. He wrote no books, constructed no church buildings, and had no monetary backing; but after 1900 years, He is the one central character of all human history. He is the pivot around which the events of the ages revolve and the only regenerator of the human race. Was it merely the Son of Joseph and Mary then who crossed the world's horizon 1900 years ago? Was it just human blood that was shed on Calvary's hill? Ah, no! What thinking man can keep from exclaiming: "My Lord, and my God!"

Fascinating, isn't it? And there is so much more. Volumes could be written on His ascension, intercession, return, and reign. Perhaps the most intriguing and fascinating thing is that He is God and yet wants to walk and talk with us. He lives in heaven and yet He wants to live with and in us. He created and owns the universe and yet He wants to be a part of our lives.

When Queen Victoria reigned in England, she occasionally visited some of the humble cottages of her subjects. After one such visit to a poor Christian widow, the neighbors of the widow taunted her by asking, "Who's the most honored guest you've entertained in your home?"

They expected her to say, "Jesus," for they recognized her deep spirituality, but to their surprise, she answered, "The most honored guest I've ever entertained is Her Majesty the Queen."

"Did you say the Queen? Ah, we caught you this time! How about this Jesus you're always talking about? Isn't He your most honored guest?"

"No, indeed," she said. "He's not a guest. He lives here."

CHAPTER 7

LIFE WITH A POWER ASSIST

A friend of mine recounts a conversation he had with a fellow passenger while flying on a plane. They were discussing "things religious" when the traveler said to my friend, "You know, if I could understand the Trinity, I think I could understand Christianity."

My friend said he was thinking about the traditional questions and the biblical answers when the fellow surprised him by saying, "I didn't have much problem thinking about God as Father, or even about Jesus Christ as being His Son, but what bothers me is the Holy Spirit. Sometimes, I think if I understood the Holy Spirit, I'd understand what the Christian life is all about."

Now, I don't think my friend, or anyone else, could explain to that fellow all about the Trinity or even all about the Christian life, but I do believe that fellow was correct. If we understood more about the Holy Spirit, we would gain a deeper understanding of the spiritual life.

You see, God gave us the Holy Spirit, among other things, to assist us in our Christian life. The Christian life is a life with a power assist! Yet today, the biblical teaching concerning the Holy Spirit is both ignored and abused. What does the Bible teach about the Holy Spirit and how does He assist believers?

The Holy Spirit is a Divine Person

A Person The Holy Spirit is often thought of as a power or influence, a misty cloud, or something nebulous. Perhaps that is because, when compared to the other members of the Trinity, He appears impersonal. God the Father is the Creator. The visible creation and the acts of creating make the personality of the Father easy to conceive. God the Son became a Man. The incarnation made His personality easy to believe, but God the Holy Spirit is somehow a secret and mystical entity. Perhaps it is because of the symbols we use to represent Him, such as wind and water, breath, a bird (a dove), and even oil and fire. Then again, maybe it is because of His name—Spirit. Somehow, people don't think of spirits as persons.

Be all of that as it may, the Holy Spirit is a person. The personal pronoun "he" is used for Him (Jn. 16:7, 8, 13-15). Twelve times in John 16:7-15, the Greek masculine pronoun he is used for the Holy Spirit. That is particularly remarkable since the Greek word for spirit is neuter, which would normally call for a neuter pronoun. Yet, contrary to normal grammatical usage, a masculine pronoun is used. This is not a pictorial personification, but a straightforward statement asserting the personality of the Holy Spirit.

On top of that, the attributes of personality are ascribed to Him. He has intelligence (1 Cor. 2:10-11), emotion (Eph. 4:30), and will (1 Cor. 12:11). Furthermore, the actions of a person are attributed to Him. In Acts 13, He communicates (Acts 13:2), calls (Acts 13:2), and commissions (Acts 13:3). More could be added, such as the names and titles used of Him implying personality, but suffice it to say, the Holy Spirit is a person.

The Bible does not make sense if the Holy Spirit is not a person. In Matthew 28:19, the disciples were told to baptize in the name of the Father, the Son, and the Holy Spirit. The first two names indicate persons. If the third is not a person, the statement loses its meaning. Imagine, "Baptize in the name of the Father and the Son and of an impersonal power." If the Holy Spirit is simply a force like the wind, Acts 15:28 would have to be rendered, "It seemed good to the wind and us." If the Holy Spirit is just a power, Acts 10:38 would have to be translated "God anointed Jesus of Nazareth with power and with power."

Years ago, R. A. Torrey said, "It is of the highest importance from the standpoint of worship that we decide whether the Holy Spirit is a divine person worthy to receive our adoration, our faith, our love, or simply an influence emanating from God or a power that God imparts to us. If the Holy Spirit is a divine person and we do not know it, we are robbing a divine being of the love and adoration that are His due. It is of the highest importance that we decide whether the Holy Spirit is a power that we, in our weakness and ignorance, are somehow to get hold of and use, or whether the Holy Spirit is a personal being, infinitely wise, infinitely holy, infinitely tender, who is to get a hold of and use us. The one concept is heathenish, the other Christian. This one concept leads to self-humiliation, self-emptying, and self-renunciation. The other concept leads to self-exaltation. It is of the highest experimental importance that we know the Holy Spirit as a person. Many can testify to the blessedness that comes into their lives when they come to know the Holy Spirit, not merely as a gracious influence (emanating, it is true, from God), but as an ever-present loving friend and helper" (Torrey, *What the Bible Teaches*, p. 225).

A Divine Person The Holy Spirit is not only a person. He is God, which is indicated by His very title. He is called the *Holy* Spirit (Acts 5:3), the Spirit of the Lord (Acts 5:9), and is acknowledged as deity (Acts 5:3-4).

His associations also prove His deity. He is associated with the other members of the Trinity (Mt. 28:19; 1 Cor. 12:4-6). Furthermore, He possesses the attributes and actions of a deity. He is said to be omniscient (1 Cor. 2:10-11), omnipotent (Gen. 1:2) and omnipresent (Ps. 139:7-10), as well as holy (Acts 5:3). He was involved in the creation of the world (Gen. 1:2), in begetting Jesus (Lk. 1:35), in the acts of regeneration (Jn. 3:5-6), and in the sanctifying of believers (2 Thess. 2:13).

Therefore, the Holy Spirit is God. He is coexistent, coequal, and coeternal with the Father and with the Son. The deity of the Holy Spirit is not a major issue today. If people accept the doctrine of the Trinity, they automatically assume the personality and deity of the Holy Spirit; however, this assumption has been a point of contention in the past.

About AD 318 in Alexandria, a man named Arius started teaching that the Father alone was God. Christ, in his view, was a created being and so was the Holy Spirit. This resulted in one of the most significant controversies in the history of the church. Councils were called; debates raged. Arianism, as it was called, was branded as a heresy. From that day to this, orthodox Christianity has affirmed the deity and personality of the Holy Spirit. As Charles Hodge says, "Since the fourth century, His true divinity has never been denied by those who admit His personality" (Hodge, *Systematic Theology*, vol. 1, p. 527).

The Work of the Holy Spirit

The Bible reveals that the Holy Spirit has done and is doing many things in relation to the universe and humanity. For example, He moved men to write the Scripture. The following is a brief survey of what He does regarding believers.

Regenerates (Titus 3:5) The theological definition of regeneration is "to impart new life." The popular expression is "born again." All humans were born spiritually dead (Eph. 2:1). Upon hearing the good news that Jesus Christ died for sin and arose from the dead, upon being convicted, enlightened, and drawn by the Holy Spirit, and upon putting their faith in Jesus Christ, people are born again. At that point, the Holy Spirit imparts new life to them (2 Pet. 1:23-25). The life He imparts is God's life (2 Pet. 1:4), an eternal kind of life (Jn. 1:13; 3:15). Therefore, the definition of the doctrine of regeneration is: At the moment of conversion, the Holy Spirit imparts new life to the believer (Titus 3:5).

Regeneration is not reformation; it is transformation. Once upon a time, a man had a pet pig who ate slop and wallowed in the mud. The problem was that the pig wanted to live in the house with his master. So, occasionally, after wallowing in the mud, he would go through the back door and make himself at home on the living room sofa. The master wanted to teach him not to sit in mud and then sit on his couch. He tried everything, including lectures, lashes, and a leash. Nothing worked. It's tough to reform a pig.

Suppose that by some supernatural power, the master could put the nature of a sheep inside his pet pig. The pig would be transformed. He would have a new kind of life, bringing new types of desires. Then, he would have to be taught how to follow the inclinations of his new life, rather than those of his old one.

A Marxist, speaking in Hyde Park, pointed to a man in rags and exclaimed, "Communism can put a new suit of clothes on that man!" A nearby Christian responded, "Christ can put a new man in that suit!"

Indwells (Jn. 14:17; 1 Cor. 6:19). The Holy Spirit moves in and takes up residence in the believer's life.

When people move into a new house, one of the first things they do is clean it. Similarly, the Bible speaks of the washing of regeneration (Titus 3:5). With the new life, there is a bath, and then the Holy Spirit moves into His new dwelling. The body of the believer is the temple of the Holy Spirit.

Seals (Eph. 1:13) At the moment of conversion, the Holy Spirit seals the believer. "In Him, you also *trusted,* after you heard the word of truth, the gospel of your salvation; in whom also, having believed, you were sealed with the Holy Spirit of promise" (Eph. 1:13). Ephesians 4:30 indicates that the Holy Spirit remains until the day of redemption when Christ returns to redeem our bodies.

The sealing work of the Holy Spirit indicates and illustrates several things: 1) Security, like a seal. When a letter is sealed, it is secured, especially if it is an important letter, such as a registered letter. 2) Protection, like the seal of a branding iron. A cattle brand on a Texas longhorn serves as a sign of identification, indicating which ranch it belongs to, and also provides protection. 3) Promise, like the seal of an engagement ring. When a fellow gives a girl that sparkling diamond ring, it carries a great sense of promise. That's one of the reasons she is so excited about it. There are good things ahead.

Human seals can be broken. A dishonest person can break the seal of a letter, a thief can steal a Texas longhorn, and a fickle fiancé can break an engagement. True, but the seal of the Holy Spirit is God's seal. He does not renege on His promises (Heb. 13:5).

Baptizes (1 Cor. 12:13). The doctrine of the baptism of the Holy Spirit is a concept that is greatly misunderstood today. The only passage in the Bible to explain it is 1 Corinthians 12:13, which says, "For by one Spirit were we all baptized into one body—whether Jews or Greeks, whether slaves or free—and have all been made to drink into one Spirit." This verse suggests that the baptism of the Holy Spirit is an action that the Holy Spirit performs.

The problem is that the Gospels make it sound like Jesus does it. John the Baptist said, "I indeed baptize you with water unto repentance, but He who is coming after me is mightier than I, whose sandals I am not worthy to carry, He will baptize you with the Holy Spirit and fire" (Mt. 3:11). Now, who does it? Jesus or the Holy Spirit?

The answer is both. It is like saying the robber killed three people in the bank with his gun and later saying that with one gun, three people were killed. Who did it? The robber or the gun? The answer is both. Likewise, Jesus baptizes people into His body through the Holy Spirit.

First Corinthians 12:13 also teaches that all are baptized into the body of Christ. Some teach that by one Spirit, *some* Christians are baptized into the body of Christ. They teach that not all believers receive the baptism of the Holy Spirit at the time of conversion, but rather *after* conversion. By saying "all," Paul indicates that all believers receive the baptism of the Holy Spirit *at the time of conversion*. Remember, this is said to a group guilty of gross sins, factions, and defections from the faith, namely, the believers at Corinth. Besides, Ephesians 1:3 says that we are blessed with *all* spiritual blessings.

The result of the baptism of the Holy Spirit is that the individual is placed into the body of Christ (see "one body" in 1 Cor. 12:13). Thus, they are permanently united to Christ and to each other. It is this point that Paul picks up on and develops in 1 Corinthians 12. Believers are one body; they are united, which means they need each other, help one another, and all hurt when one of them is hurt. The definition of the baptism of the Holy Spirit is that, at the moment of conversion, Jesus Christ and the Holy Spirit place the believer into the body of Christ (1 Cor. 12:13).

When people have a toothache, other members of their body feel the pain. They may even decide to do nothing with the tooth. Their hands, their feet, their arms, and their legs could get together for a conference and decide, "This is not *our* problem. We will have nothing to do with that painful tooth," but the fact is, when one member of the body was kept awake all night, all members stayed awake. Likewise, when one Christian hurts, all Christians hurt because they're all members of the same body.

When other members of a person's body realize that the aching tooth is going to affect them, they will all take part in helping. The feet and the legs carry the individual to the medicine cabinet. The arms and the hands see to it that the medicine gets to the tooth. Even the fingers get in on the act.

The Holy Spirit has put believers into the body of Christ. They are part of Him and part of each other. One part of the body is in pain, and the other parts are not, which indicates a sick or even deformed function of the body.

Enables Having given believers new life and taken up residence in them, as well as sealing them and placing them into the body of Christ, the Holy Spirit is now in a position to enable them to live the Christian life. Galatians 5:16 says, "This I say, then, walk in the Spirit, and you shall not fulfill the lusts of the flesh." How is that done?

First, if people are to walk in the Spirit, they must know where to walk, at least in what direction. The Holy Spirit is the Spirit of truth that guides us into all truth (Jn. 16:13). This truth refers to the Word of God (Jn. 17:17), through which the Holy Spirit communicates to us.

The Holy Spirit not only supplies instruction, He also enables believers. Ephesians 3:16 says, "That He would grant you, according to the riches of His glory, to be strengthened with might through His Spirit in the inner man." As believers depend upon Him to do what the Word says, He enables them to accomplish the task.

Notice carefully, however, that Galatians 5:16 says, "*Walk* in the Spirit." Walking takes effort. Paul did not say, "Sit" in the Spirit. Believers have to do something. They have to put forth effort to walk. Adults take walking for granted, but learning to walk takes great effort and discipline. Walking in the Spirit requires the same. To be specific and demonstrate precisely how this works, imagine a fellow having a problem with being patient with people. The Spirit of God working in his life will guide his attention to the Word of God, showing him that God desires patience, particularly with others. Then, as he puts forth effort to be patient with others and, at the same time, depending on the Lord for grace, he will discover that God will give him the ability to exercise patience.

Summary: The Holy Spirit is the third person of the triune God (Acts 5:3, 4) who regenerates (Titus 3:5), indwells (1 Cor. 6:19), seals (Eph. 1:13), baptizes (1 Cor. 12:13), and enables the believer to obey the Word of God (Eph. 3:16).

God, in the person of the Holy Spirit, lives inside of believers and is willing to enable them to obey the Scriptures. It is life (remember regeneration) with a power assist. Simply put, believers have God's presence and God's power to implement God's precepts in their lives.

Some do not have God's presence. They are like a car without a motor. As vehicles were made to have motors placed inside, humans were created for God to dwell inside them. When an individual trusts Christ, God, in the person of the Holy Spirit, takes up residence within that person.

Others have God's presence, but they do not utilize God's power. They sometimes erroneously conclude that they need more of the Holy Spirit. Impossible! He is a person. How does one get one-half or one-tenth of a person? The individual who has trusted Christ has received all the Holy Spirit he will ever get. The issue is not, "Do you have more of the Spirit?" but "Does the Holy Spirit have more of you?"

At a meeting in Philadelphia called to discuss the possibilities of inviting D. L. Moody to conduct an evangelistic campaign there, an objector said, "Do you think that Mr. Moody has a monopoly on the Holy Spirit?" The chairman answered, "No, but the Holy Spirit seems to have a monopoly on Mr. Moody." If you are a Christian, you have the Holy Spirit within you. Does He have all of you?

CHAPTER 8

IS THE BIBLE THE WORD OF GOD?

When my children were small, we had family night once a week. We often played board games. On one occasion, my son and I disagreed over how to play the game. He insisted that it should be done one way, even though I knew it was supposed to be done another. I shared my thoughts with him, but he remained unpersuaded. His mother and sisters sided with me. He was still not moved. Finally, I noted that the game's manufacturer determined its gameplay. Get the rules and let's see what he said. We all agreed that the rules would dictate how we played the game.

People playing the game of life differ on how the game should be played. Some insist that it should be done one way, while others claim it should be done another. All of us are called upon to determine what we believe and how we should behave. How do we settle those questions for ourselves and disputes with others? Is our personal opinion all that counts? Is a majority vote the final court of appeal? Or is there a rulebook written by the manufacturer?

Christianity claims that God, the maker of heaven and earth as well as human beings, wrote a book. If so, His Word is the final word concerning doctrine and deportment. The Bible tells us what we should believe concerning God, man, salvation, the church, and the future. It also tells us how we are to behave—at home, at work, at church, toward our neighbor, and toward the government.

The Scripture has something to say about every area of life, including our thought life and sex life.

The question is, "Is the Bible the Word of God?" If the answer to that question is "Yes," what does that mean, and how do we know?

The Distinction of Inspiration

The doctrine of inspiration needs to be put into perspective. There is a difference between revelation, inspiration, and illumination. Revelation is the *giving* of truth; inspiration is the *recording* of truth; illumination is the *understanding* of truth.

Revelation There can be revelation *without* inspiration. In other words, a truth can be revealed but not recorded. The apostle Paul was transported to the third heaven. He had a revelation (2 Cor. 12:7), but it was unlawful for him to reveal it to anyone else (2 Cor. 12:4).

Inspiration It is important to note that inspiration is not revelation; it is the recording of truth from *whatever* source it was obtained. The writers of Scripture may have received direct revelation, as in the case of the Ten Commandments. They also recorded truth from their experience (Joshua), from research (Lk. 1:1-4), and even from other written material outside the Bible (Titus 1:12). In other words, to say that God inspires the Bible does not mean that God *directly* revealed everything in the Bible to men. Instead, it means that regardless of the source of their information, the Holy Spirit directed the writers in such a way that what they wrote was what God intended.

Illumination The other distinction that needs to be made is that of illumination. Illumination is the work of the Spirit of God in helping believers *understand* what is written (Eph. 1:18).

The Definition of Inspiration

What is inspiration? Paul told Timothy, "All Scripture is given by inspiration of God" (2 Tim. 3:16). The doctrine of inspiration is that God influenced the writers of Scripture so that they recorded His Word. This definition contains four concepts that need to be considered in detail.

Supernatural Inspiration First, *God* influenced the authors of Scripture. Inspiration is something that God did. The Greek word rendered "inspiration of God" in 2 Timothy 3:16 means "God-breathed." The inspiration of the Bible was supernatural.

The natural theory of inspiration denies that there was anything supernatural, mysterious, or particular in the writing of Scripture. It contends that the authors of the Bible were inspired in the same sense as Homer, Shakespeare, and Tennyson. People holding this view would say, "Were not Bach, Beethoven, and Brahms inspired?" They would say the inspired football team won the game. They would argue that just as there have been gifted (exceptional) authors and artists, poets, and players, so there can be gifted men with spiritual insight. This view emphasizes the human authorship to the exclusion of the divine.

Notice carefully that 2 Timothy 3:16 does not say that God inspired people; it says God inspired Scripture. The Bible is not the record of inspired *writers* but a record of inspired *writings*.

Dynamic Inspiration God *influenced* the authors of Scripture. Second Peter 1:21 says, "Prophecy never came by the will of men, but holy men of God spoke as the Holy Spirit moved them." The Greek word translated "moved" means "to bear along," as the wind bears along a ship. God superintended the authors of Scripture. This is called the dynamic theory of inspiration.

The mechanical view of inspiration says that God dictated and men wrote like secretaries. The authors of Scripture were nothing more than amanuenses. A few parts of the Bible were written this way. For example, God dictated the Ten Commandments to Moses.

Not all of Scripture, however, was dictated. That is obvious because of the differences in style between the books of the Bible. The Scripture clearly contains the human authors' identities, individualities, and idiosyncrasies. Isaiah was a brilliant court preacher who penned eloquent poetry and prose. Amos was a country preacher. His writings have the smell of a newly plowed furrow of soil. The highly educated Paul used sophisticated words and the unschooled John used simple language. We must conclude, therefore, that from God's point of view, the Holy Spirit gave through men what He wished to record. Yet, from the human point of view, communication came forth in a language such as men themselves would have naturally chosen. In the final analysis, the doctrine of inspiration is a mystery!

Scissors are an illustration. A seamstress makes a cut in cloth with scissors with a long blade, scissors with a short blade, or pinking shears. Each pair of scissors made a different cut. It could be said that the scissors did it. At the same time, the seamstress is the one to choose to use that pair at that place in the cloth. Likewise, the different authors of Scripture manifest distinctive "cuts," but God was using all to make what He wanted.

Verbal Inspiration Human authors wrote God's Word. The Holy Spirit teaches words (Ex. 20:1; Jn. 6:63; 17:8; 1 Cor. 2:12-13). This is known as verbal inspiration.

Concept inspiration claims that only the concepts or thoughts of the Bible are inspired. According to this view, God imparted ideas that left human authors free to express them in their own language. The problem with this view is that it overlooks the fact that thoughts cannot exist independently of words. It also ignores the immeasurably essential words in any message. The Bible does not hesitate to hinge a whole argument on one word. Jesus Himself based an argument for His deity on one word (Mt. 22:44-45). Paul based an argument on the difference between a singular and a plural (Gal. 3:16).

Words are important. A single word can change a message. Years ago, a man purchased a large number of goods from a New York merchant, who gave him a note promising payment and a well-known firm in Chicago as a reference. A telegram was sent to verify the promise. The answer received was "Note good for any amount." The goods were delivered, but payment was never received. Upon investigation, it was revealed that the telegram should have read "Not good for any amount." Through carelessness, "not" was changed to "note." One letter made a big difference to one New York merchant. One word can make the difference between accurately and inaccurately conveying a message.

Changing one word could change the message of the Bible. In an early edition of the King James Version of the Bible (1631), a printer inadvertently left out the word "not" in Exodus 20:14. The result was that Exodus 20:14 read, "You shall commit adultery." Recently, a study Bible was printed and distributed. A note in Leviticus read, "Moral purity is extremely destructive to spiritual life and personal relationships." It should have read, "Moral impurity." Changing one word can make a big difference.

Plenary Inspiration: "His Word" implies and includes all of His Words. This is commonly referred to as plenary inspiration. Partial inspiration says that only parts of the Bible are inspired. Some have rejected the book of Esther. Today, this theory is expressed by the sentence, "The Bible *contains* the Word of God."

The problem with this view is that it makes human reason the judge of what is inspired and what is not. Some people believe the Bible is inspired in spots and they are inspired to pick out the spots.

The Bible teaches a supernatural, dynamic, verbal, plenary inspiration. It does not teach a natural, mechanical, conceptual, or partial inspiration. In short, all Scripture is God-breathed.

The Defense of Inspiration

How do we know the Bible is inspired? After all, other books claim inspiration too. The *Koran* says, "This Koran cannot have been composed by any except by God.... There is no doubt, thereof, it is sent down from the Lord of all creatures" (*Koran*, chapter 10).
The Claim First of all, the Bible claims to be the Word of God. The words "God said" occur ten times in the first chapter of Genesis. Moses, the author of the first five books of the Bible, claimed God spoke to him (Lev. 1:1; etc.) and that God told him to write down what He said (Ex. 17:14; 24:2-4). When Moses died, God told his successor, Joshua, to hear and heed what Moses wrote (Jos. 1:7-8). The prophets in the Old Testament made similar claims (Isa. 1:1; Jer. 1:1; Ezek. 1:1; Hosea 1:1; Joel 1:1; Amos 1:3; Obad. 1; Jonah 1:1; Micah 1:1; Nahum 1:1; Hab. 1:1; Zeph. 1:1; Haggai 1:1; Zach. 1:1; Mal. 1:1). The prophets claimed God spoke to them and they spoke for God. The Old Testament, then, clearly claims to be the Word of God. It is said that such expressions as

"the Lord said," "the Lord spoke," and "the Word of the Lord came" are found 3,808 times in the Old Testament. Furthermore, the New Testament claims the Old Testament is the Word of God (Heb. 1:1; 2 Pet. 1:20-21).

The New Testament also claims that it is the Word of God. As Moses and the prophets claimed to speak for God, so did Paul (1 Cor. 14:37), John (Rev. 1:10, 11, 19), and Peter (2 Pet. 3:1-2). Moreover, Peter acknowledges that Paul's writings were Scripture (2 Pet. 3:15-16) and Paul quotes Luke, calling what Luke wrote Scripture (1 Tim. 5:18).

The point is that the Bible claims to be the Word of God (2 Tim. 3:16). Some take exception to the logic that since the Bible claims to be the Word of God, it is. They call this a circular argument. Granted, logically, just because the Bible claims to be God's Word doesn't mean it is. Candidly, it only means that it *may* be the Word of God. It doesn't necessarily mean it *must* be, but it sure means it *could* be. In a court of law, a defendant has the right to engage in self-testimony. His testimony may not be true, but if he should refuse to testify, it would surely make the jury skeptical. A fair and impartial jury wants to hear what the defendant says.

A circular argument would be if the defendant said, "I'm not guilty," and, as a result, the judge immediately ruled that he was innocent. It is not a circular argument if additional testimony is allowed and evaluated to determine the credibility of the defendant's testimony. Nevertheless, the defendant's testimony is permitted in court. Likewise, the testimony of Scripture concerning itself does not settle the matter, but its testimony should at least be heard.

The claim of the Scripture that it is inspired does prove one thing. Some argue that the Bible is not God's book, but it is a good book. If the Bible is not God's book, it cannot be good because it claims to be God's book. If it is not, it is lying; therefore, it is not good. Any book that tells 3,808 lies is not a good book; it is a bad book.

Many arguments have been used to defend the doctrine of inspiration. Dr. R. A. Torrey wrote a booklet entitled *Ten Reasons Why I Believe the Bible is the Word of God*. Another booklet brags *Fifty-seven Reasons Why We Know the Bible is the Word of God*. There is both objective and subjective evidence that the Bible is God's Word.

The Objective Evidence Besides the fact that the Bible claims to be the Word of God, the consistency of the Bible is an example of objective evidence. The consistency of the Scripture is astounding. The writing of the Bible took about 1,500 years, from 1,400 BC to AD 95. More than 40 different authors wrote the sixty-six books of the Bible. It was written by kings such as David and Solomon, by statesmen such as Daniel and Nehemiah, by priests such as Ezra, by men learned in the wisdom of Egypt such as Moses, by men learned in Jewish law such as Paul, a herdsman such as Amos, a tax collector such as Matthew, fishermen such as Peter, James, and John, a physician such as Luke and such mighty prophets as Isaiah, Ezekiel, and Zechariah. In some cases, the authors were not contemporaries and had no way of comparing notes with each other, yet their writings were completely consistent and contained no contradictions.

Another part of the objective evidence for inspiration is fulfilled prophecy. The Bible contains many predictions that later were fulfilled. For example, Isaiah 13 foretold the destruction of Babylon by the Medes. This prophecy was given during the reign of Hezekiah, who ruled about 726 BC. At the time, the Medes were

Medes were not even a nation. They were only a roving band of mountain tribes subject to the kings of Assyria. It was not until 607 BC, when Cyaxares overthrew Nineveh, that they began to exert power, and not until the revolt of Cyrus in 550 BC did they become a power with which to be reckoned. Predicting that the Medes would destroy Babylon is akin to forecasting that the Sioux Indians would defeat America in the year AD 2050. We know that there are Sioux Indians, whereas when Isaiah wrote, he didn't know about the Medes. The only reasonable conclusion is that this information was given supernaturally.

Or consider the prophecies concerning the coming of the Messiah. Hundreds of years before Jesus came, it was predicted in the Old Testament that the Messiah would be a descendant of David (2 Sam. 7:12), that He would be born in Bethlehem (Micah 5:2), and that He would be born of a virgin (Isa. 7:14). Even His arrival time was prophesied (Dan. 9:25-26). All these and many more prophecies concerning the coming of the Messiah were fulfilled meticulously.

The proof of inspiration is fulfilled prophecy. No other book can claim the prophetic predictions that the Bible can. It is simply astounding and must be supernatural.

The Subjective Evidence There is also subjective evidence that the Bible is from God. It has spoken to people all over the world for centuries. There is a distinct spiritual atmosphere that sets the Bible apart from every other book, including other religious texts that claim to convey a divine message. J. B. Phillips, who translated and published a paraphrased version of the New Testament, said that when he began the translation of the New Testament epistles, he was constantly struck by their vitality and power. "Again and again, as I carried out my translation, I felt like an electrician who was rewiring an ancient house without being able to turn the mains off." The Bible has something that sets it apart from every other book in the world. For this reason, a Stone Age Indian in South America exclaimed when he heard for the first time a portion of Scripture translated in his own language, "Ah, that Book, it speaks to my stomach."

It has spoken to me. If it has not spoken to you, you will have a hard time accepting this argument. In fact, it would be difficult, if not impossible, to explain this to you. It would be like me trying to tell you what an orange tastes like if you'd never tasted one.

Summary: There is objective and subjective proof that the Bible is the Word of God; that is, God supernaturally, yet dynamically and verbally, wrote His Word through men.

So what? In a word, authorship determines authority. When I pick up a book to read, one of the first things I do is check to see who wrote it. I want to know if the author is qualified to speak on the subject of the book. Sometimes, I recognize the author's name immediately. If I don't know enough about the author to satisfy myself that the author is qualified, I may proceed cautiously. If I don't recognize the name or anything about the author's reputation or right to speak on the subject, I investigate. The investigation usually leads me to the dust cover. There, I can uncover evidence to demonstrate the author's qualifications. One of the frustrations of some books is the lack of information about the author and the absence of a dust cover. Knowing who wrote the book is important. It determines whether or not the author has the authority to speak on the subject of the book.

In the case of the Bible, if humans and only humans wrote it, people might read it for its literary value and follow it if they wish and only when they wish. If the Bible is not the Word of God, people must, to use the words of Plato, "Take the best and most irrefutable of human theories and let this be the raft upon which he sails on life, not without risk, unless he can find some word of God which will more surely and safely carry him." If the Bible is not God's Word, its teachings join the babbling opinions of people.

On the other hand, if it is, in truth, the Word of God, we must read it and heed it, for authorship determines authority. Suppose the Bible is, in fact, the Word of God. In that case, it has authority over my opinion, the traditions of men, the majority vote of a group, the reasoning of philosophers, the pronouncements of kings, and the theories of anybody, including so-called scientists.

Believers in Jesus Christ are quick to affirm the inspiration of the Scriptures, but then they neutralize and negate what God says by their rationalizations, traditions, and theories. If the Bible is the Word of God, I have no choice but to believe that there is a God. I cannot be an atheist or agnostic. I must believe in the Trinity. I cannot be a Unitarian. I must believe in the deity, death, and resurrection of Jesus Christ. I cannot be a skeptic. I must believe that human beings were created in the image of God and yet have fallen into sin and need a Savior. I cannot be an evolutionist. I must believe that salvation is by grace through faith in Jesus Christ. I cannot simply be a good person or a religious person, and I hope to get to heaven through my actions. I must believe that God's institution today is His church. I cannot be a non-church-goer or just be involved in a para-church ministry. I must believe that Jesus Christ is coming back, just as He ascended. I cannot be non-committal concerning future events prophesied in the Bible.

That is only the beginning. Christians are fond of saying that the Bible is the final authority for faith and practice. If the Bible is indeed the Word of God, I must love God, love my neighbor as myself, and love other believers as Jesus Christ loved me. I cannot be unloving. I must forgive all, including my enemies. I cannot be unforgiving. I must be committed to becoming more and more like Jesus Christ and making Him more and more known in the world. I cannot be uncommitted.

If the Bible is, in truth, the Word of God, believers in Jesus Christ must read and heed it, for authorship determines authority. If you were a soldier in a battle and a private cried, "Charge!" you probably wouldn't move, but if a general ordered, "Charge!" you would be obligated to obey. Authorship determines authority. The Lord of Lords, the King of Kings, the General of Generals has spoken. Are you listening?

CHAPTER 9

HOW TO UNDERSTAND THE WHOLE BIBLE

Mitch, a hard-shell Baptist, loved to sneak away to the racetrack. One day, he was betting on the ponies and nearly lost his shirt when he noticed a priest who stepped out onto the track and blessed the forehead of one of the horses lining up for the fourth race. Lo and behold, this very long-shot horse won the race. Mitch was most interested in seeing what the priest did in the next race.

Sure enough, the priest stepped onto the track as the fifth race horses lined up and placed his blessing on the forehead of one of the horses. Mitch made a beeline for the window and placed a small bet on the horse. Again, even though it was another long shot, the horse won the race. Mitch collected his winnings and anxiously waited to see which horse the priest bestowed his blessing on for the sixth race. The priest blessed a horse, Mitch bet on it, and it won! Mitch was elated!

As the day went on, the priest continued blessing one of the horses, and it always came in first. Mitch began to pull in some serious money, and by the last race, he knew his wildest dreams would come true. He quickly stopped at the ATM, withdrew big money, and waited for the priest's blessing to tell him which horse to bet on. True to his pattern, the priest stepped onto the track and blessed one of the horses' foreheads, eyes, ears, and hooves. Mitch bet every cent and watched the horse come in dead last.

Mitch was dumbfounded. He made his way to the track and when he found the priest, he demanded, "What happened, Father? All day, you blessed horses and they won. In the last race, you blessed a horse and he lost. Now I've lost my savings, thanks to you!!" The priest nodded wisely and said, "That's the problem with you Protestants ... you can't tell the difference between a simple blessing and the Last Rites."

Similarly, some people cannot distinguish between the different parts of the Bible. For example, some read the Ten Commandments and decide to observe the Sabbath. Is that true? Or are there distinctions they are not making?

When I became a Christian at age 18, I did not understand anything—at all—about the Bible. I did not know Genesis was the first book and Revelation was the last. I was unfamiliar with John 3:16 until I saw it in print, where I wondered why a colon was placed between the 3 and the 16. I was so ignorant of the Bible that I thought the New Testament was written in the twentieth century. It is new. The Old Testament was written in the first century. It is old. When I first discovered that the life of Christ was recorded in the New Testament, I was shocked! I knew nothing about the Bible!

Then, the Pastor, who led me to Christ, explained something to me that enabled me to understand the Bible at once. What he did was simple, short, and sufficient to explain many things I encountered in Scripture.

What he shared with me is called dispensationalism. The Greek word "dispensation" comes from the Greek word for "administrator," which means "the manager of a house or an estate." The idea is that, like a household administrator, God has administered His program on the earth. It would be more accurate to say He has administered His programs on earth because He has changed His program occasionally. These "administrations" or "programs" are called dispensations.

Parents manage their household and children, yet they still change the program. When children are between the ages of 1 and 6, they go to bed at 8:00 p.m. When they are 16, they get to stay up until 11:00 p.m. Children go through dispensations.

It is evident God has changed His program. In Romans 5:13-14, Paul distinguishes between the period between Adam and Moses and the period after Moses. Paul says that those between Adam and Moses did not sin as Adam did (Rom. 5:14); that is, Adam was given a specific prohibition and those after Adam until Moses were not given a law. Paul's point is that even though there was no law between Adam and Moses, people were still sinners because sin produces death, and they died (Rom. 5:14). Clearly, God changed His program from no law to the Mosaic Law.

Another indication that God has changed His program is given in the first chapter of John's Gospel. John says, "For the law was given through Moses, but grace and truth came through Jesus Christ." That statement at least implies a change in the program.

How many times has God changed His program? In other words, how many dispensations are there? There are at least three. Paul speaks of a former dispensation (Col. 1:25-26), of the dispensation of the grace of God, which was given to him concerning the church (Eph. 3:2), and of a dispensation of the fullness of time, which is to come in the future (Eph. 1:10).

Most Dispensationalists further divide the past dispensation into several others until they end up with seven dispensations, including Innocence, Conscience, Human Government, Promise, Law, Grace, and the Future Millennium of a 1000-year reign of

Christ on the earth. They have a valid point. There was a different program before Adam sinned (Innocence) than after (Conscience). Sometime after the fall, God instituted human government and then promised that the seed of the patriarchs would inherit the land, all of which was the program before the Mosaic law was instituted. Of the seven dispensations, some are short and minor, and others are long and major. For simplicity's sake, the seven can be summarized into four.

The Dispensation of the Gentiles

The Name In the first dispensation, which can be called the dispensation of the Gentiles, God did not deal with one nation, like Israel, or one group, like the church. Instead, He dealt with all human beings. He dealt with the Gentiles (Gen. 1-11).

The Program God's program, that is, people's responsibility during this dispensation, included innocence, conscience, and human government. As long as Adam and Eve were in the Garden, their responsibility was to be fruitful (Gen. 1:28), subdue the earth (Gen. 1:28), care for the Garden (Gen. 2:15), and not eat of the tree of the knowledge of good and evil (Gen. 2:17). Adam failed and thus fell.

After the Garden experience, man was told to till the ground. There was no code or law, just conscience and a limited revelation from God. People, however, rebelled again and manifested their sinfulness. This time, Cain killed Abel. From there, it was downhill until things got so bad that God brought the judgment of the Flood. He then instituted government, instructing that a killer was to be killed (Gen. 9:6).

Dispensationalism helps clarify the Scriptures. For example, Cain killed Abel, but he was not killed because God had not yet revealed the principle of capital punishment. In other words, Cain was in another dispensation. By the way, the first responsibility of human government was capital punishment, a concept that should be practiced even in this dispensation (Rom. 13:4).

The Dispensation of the Jews

The Name In the next broad dispensation, God dealt with the Jews. That does not mean He dealt with them exclusively, but rather that He dealt with them primarily. They were to be His witnesses to the world. At the same time, He dealt with Gentiles, such as Ruth, the Queen of Sheba, and Nineveh (Genesis 12 through Malachi and the Gospels).

The Program People's responsibility during this administration of God's program could be summed up in promise and law.

God promised Abraham that He would make his descendants a great nation and bless others through him (Gen. 12:1-3). Abraham believed God and it was accounted to him for righteousness (Gen. 15:6). That promise is still in effect (Gal. 3:16-17).

Years later, God gave the Law to Moses. That legal system was added to the promise given to Abraham until the coming of Christ (Gal. 3:19; Jn. 1:17).

Although the Bible views the Mosaic Law as a unit, it can be said that it consists of 1) commandments, which were moral laws (Ex. 20:1-26), 2) judgments, which were civil and social laws (Ex. 21:1-24:11), and 3) ordinances, which were religious codes (Ex. 24:12-31:18). This third category included the Tabernacle with its sacrifices, the feasts and their ceremonies, and the judgments with their limitations.

It must be noted carefully that the Mosaic system has ended (Gal. 3:19). Believers in the church dispensation do not sacrifice lambs or live by Old Testament regulations and limitations, including worshiping on Saturday (Gal. 4:9-10).

That does not mean we should rip the Old Testament from our Bibles and throw it away. While it is true that the Old Testament does not apply to believers in this dispensation, believers can still learn from it (1 Cor. 10:11; Rom. 15:4). The Old Testament was not written *to* believers, but it was written *for* them.

Cruising down the highway, you may see a police officer writing out a ticket to a speeder. That ticket was not written *to* you but *for* you as an example and an admonition.

The Dispensation of the Church

The Name In the third broad basic dispensation, God deals with the church. In a sense, He ceases to deal with the Jews, at least temporarily. He will deal with them again as a nation in the future (Rom. 11). Yet, in another sense, God is now dealing with Jews and Gentiles, that is, individuals who trust Christ. In other words, God is dealing with the church (Acts through Revelation 3).

The Program People's responsibility during this dispensation could be summed up in the word "grace." God ended the legal system and now deals with His children by grace (Jn. 1:17). That does not mean that God did not exercise grace in the Mosaic legal system. That system is now eliminated and God deals with His children solely by grace, apart from the Mosaic legal system. In this dispensation, as in the old dispensation, people are saved by grace (Eph. 2:8). Christians are to grow by grace (2 Pet. 3:18) and serve by grace (Titus 2:11-12).

When some Christians hear that dispensationalists claim that we are under grace and not law, they immediately object, feeling that it makes Christians lawless. Their logic sometimes goes like this: Moses said, "Do not kill." If we're not under Moses' Law, we can kill, right?

Granted, believers today are under grace and not the Mosaic Law, but perhaps it might be more accurate to say that they are under the Law of Christ and not under the Law of Moses. Christ's Law is the law of love. A comparison of the two "laws" reveals that some of the laws are the same and some are different. Murder is a case mentioned under both systems. Moses said, "You shall not murder" (Ex. 20:13). The Law of Christ agrees, for if you love, you will not murder or commit adultery (Rom. 13:9-10).

Nevertheless, some of the items in the two systems are different. Moses said, "You shall keep the Sabbath day holy" (Ex. 20:8). The New Testament says that those laws engraved in stone, which would include the Sabbath day, have been done away with (2 Cor. 3:7). So, it is no surprise that when Paul lists specific commandments under the law of love that he eliminates Sabbath-keeping (Rom. 13:8-10). When one group of first-century Christians wanted to keep some of the Old Testament laws, including Sabbath observance, Paul told them that they desired again to be in bondage (Gal. 4:9-10).

Let me illustrate. I once lived in Texas. They had a law that stated, "Don't murder." Then I moved to Tennessee. Therefore, I was no longer under Texas law, and if I had killed someone in Tennessee, the Texas police would not and could not have arrested me. Does that mean then that I was free to kill? Of course not! I was under Tennessee law and that state also had a law against murder. When it came to the subject of murder, both states had the same law.

There were other areas, however, in which they differed. At the time (1966), the Texas speed limit was 70 mph on the open highway, and the Tennessee speed limit was 75 mph. I could drive faster in Tennessee. I was not as restricted, but that does not mean that I was lawless. Likewise, there is a sense in which God's children, under grace, have more freedom, but that does not mean they are lawless.

The Dispensation of Christ

The Name The future dispensation is often called the Kingdom or the Millennium; it could be called the dispensation of Christ. During this administration, God will deal with people through the personal presence of Christ, ruling and reigning on the earth (Rev. 20).

It should be pointed out in passing that between the dispensation of grace and the dispensation of the kingdom, several things will happen, including the Rapture, the Tribulation, and the Second Coming. These will be dealt with in the chapter on prophecy.

The Program People's responsibility during the dispensation of Christ will be to obey the King, who will rule with a rod of iron (Rev. 19:15). Frankly, during that time, there will be a dictatorship, which is probably the best form of government. It is efficient. Today's problem with this type of government is the nature of the leaders at the top. When the God/Man is the "man on top," that problem is solved. Christ will be a just, fair, and benevolent dictator.

Summary: God has administered His program through the centuries, and that program has changed.

Dispensationalism is the doctrine that God has used different programs to accomplish His purpose (Eph. 3:2; 1:10). To understand the Bible, one must grasp this concept. While all theologians are willing to admit that God's program, or at least some details of it, have changed through the ages, not all are dispensationalists in the theological sense of the term. Technically, dispensationalists insist that God has one program for Israel and another for the church. In other words, they make a distinction between Israel and the church.

Many have criticized dispensationalism, accusing it of teaching two ways of salvation. God's program has changed; His plan of salvation has not. It has always been salvation by grace through faith (Rom. 4:1-6). Abraham, David, Paul, and people are all saved by grace through faith.

The plan of salvation has always been the same. The program after salvation, however, has changed. Dr. Lewis Sperry Chafer used to say, "If you do not take a lamb to the Tabernacle on Saturday, you are a dispensationalist."

Personally, dispensationalism has helped me to understand the Bible more than anything else. Recognizing God's program, and especially the fact that His program has changed from time to time, is an immense aid in keeping things straight in the Bible.

For example, we do not keep Saturdays because we are not under Mosaic Law. On the other hand, God's program, for now, is building His church, the body of Christ. If you are in sync with what God is doing, you will be involved in that process.

Or, to put that same thing another way, if you do not understand where you are in the program of God, you can jump to the wrong conclusions. Suppose you went to a three-act musical play. At the beginning of the program, they announced that in Act Two, the audience would participate in a sing-along for one song. Then, suppose you fell asleep or went to get some popcorn. At any rate, you lost your place in the program and you wanted to sing along. So, at some point, you started singing with the actors, which happened to be in the middle of Act Three. You can easily fall out of sync if you're unsure where you are in the program.

CHAPTER 10

THE BIBLICAL VIEW OF YOU

What are human beings? The biological view considers humans to be primarily complex biological animals. Yet people are different from animals. Animals can be tool users; people are toolmakers. Behaviorists have a mechanical view of human beings. According to them, people react to events in their environment like a typewriter reacts to fingers pounding on its keys.

Answers range from one extreme to the other, with many variations in between. On one end of the spectrum are those who say people are good. Psychologist Carl Rogers would say that humans are not negative; they are only positive. All that is within is good. Corruption enters from outside of people.

On the other extreme are those who say people are basically bad. No less than Sigmund Freud said that people's primary motivation is self-gratification. They are basically out for themselves. According to him, there are two basic drives pressing for gratification: the drive toward sexual pleasure (eros) and the drive toward power and destruction (thanatos).

Then, there are those in between. B. F. Skinner contends that people are neither good nor bad. According to Skinner, they are complicated masses of responses. They are controlled beings.

Existentialists don't know if people are bad (Freud), good (Rogers), both, or neither (Skinner). To them, humans are logically absurd (Larry Crabb, *Basic Principles of Biblical Counseling*, p. 41).

What is the biblical view of you? The biblical doctrine of people is usually divided into two major parts: dignity and depravity.

Dignity

Image of God When God created people, He said, "Let us make man in our image, according to Our likeness" (Gen. 1:26). The Hebrew word translated "image" means "image, likeness, resemblance." The word translated "likeness" means "likeness or similitude." The second phrase is merely supplementary or explanatory of the first. Therefore, they do not refer to two different things. The two words are used interchangeably to express the idea that people were created in the very image of God. God made people not only according to His plan but according to the pattern of His person. Coins are stamped from a die. When you examine a coin, you can tell what was engraved in the die because the coin bears the image of the die that pressed it. Likewise, people bear the resemblance of God. The question is, "What is the likeness?"

Not Physical A common misconception is that people are created in the image of God, comprising body, soul, and spirit. The Mormons actually teach that. Joseph Smith said, "There is no other God in heaven but that God who has flesh and bones." According to Mormonism, God the Father has a body, and when the Bible says He created man in His image, the image includes a body.

The phrase "the image of God" does not include the body, for God is spirit (Jn. 4:24) and a spirit does not have flesh and bones (Lk. 24:39). God is invisible (Col. 1:15). Remember also that God forbade images for the simple reason that there was nothing in the earth that could resemble Him (Deut. 4:15-19).

Holiness If the image of God in people does not include the body, what does it include? Theologians have debated this question for centuries. One of the most common suggestions is that since God is holy and people have His image, they have the capacity for holiness. There seems to be support for this view in Ephesians 4:24. After salvation, the new person is created after God in righteousness and true holiness.

There is a difference, of course, between the holiness that believers have today and the holiness that Adam had before the Fall. Martin Luther said, "I understand this image of God to be ... that Adam not only knew God and believed in Him that was gracious; but that he also led an entirely godly life." Ryrie calls Adam's holiness "unconfirmed holiness" and our holiness "confirmed holiness."

Whether or not Ephesians 4:24 proves that the image of God in people is the capacity for holiness, this much is certain. Before the fall, Adam had fellowship with God, but the animals did not. Adam was a spiritual being with spiritual capacities.

Even if the capacity for holiness view is correct, it does not explain everything. After the Fall, people retained the image of God, at least to some degree (Gen. 9:6; 2 Cor. 11:7), but they were not holy. Therefore, simply stating that the image is holy does not tell the whole story.

Personhood That observation has driven many to conclude that the image involves personhood, that is, God is a person (a being with mind, emotions, and will). Thus, when people were created in His image, they, too, had intellectual power, natural affection, and moral freedom. They at least had sufficient intelligence to give names to all the animals (Gen. 2:19-20). Adam could think, reason, and speak. He could attach words to ideas. Humans did not lose these capacities after the Fall.

Colossians 3:10 seems to support this view. After salvation, the new person is created with knowledge after the image of God who created him. Calvin said, "There is no doubt that the proper seat of His image is in the soul."

The image of God in people, then, is not physical but spiritual and primarily in His personhood. Children are often said to be "just like" their father or mother. That can be physical, like the features of their face, but it can also be non-physical, like their personality. I have three children, each with traits that mirror my own. The one characteristic people comment about the most is that one of them has my personality. It is often said, "Your oldest daughter is just like you." She is outgoing, fun-loving, and talks a lot. She is made in my image, but that is not physical; it is non-physical.

A definition of the doctrine of the dignity of people is: Humans were created in the image of God and, thus, have a capacity for holiness and personality (Gen. 1:26; Eph. 4:24; Col. 3:10).

People are made in the image of God, an image which remains, at least to some degree, even after the Fall. People have dignity. The Bible applies this truth in two specific areas. It tells us that since people are created in the image of God, they should not commit murder (Gen. 9:6), nor should they slander (Jas. 3:9). Since people are made in the image of God, they should not destroy one another, either with a gun or with gossip.

We should treat all humans with dignity. In the TV show *Law and Order,* a police officer asked to be taken off a case because the man who was murdered had a lifestyle that was repugnant to him. His superior refused, saying that no matter what a person has done, they should be treated with dignity. He went on to say that a crime had been committed and it needs to be investigated regardless of the people involved.

This concept also applies to you. The biblical view of you is that you are made in the image of God and, therefore, have dignity. Some people think too lowly of themselves. Because of the way they have been treated or the way they have behaved, they think of themselves as worthless worms. You have worth and dignity; you have been created in the image of God.

Depravity

The second major thing the Bible teaches about people is that they are sinful; they are depraved. What does that mean? How depraved is this depravity?

Total Depravity Some say people are not depraved at all. Liberals would say that humans are made in the image of God and are, therefore, good. Others believe in partial depravity. According to this view, humans are half well and half sick. If they cooperated with God, they would be righteous. This view teaches that people are affected by the Fall, but not to the extent that they are incapable of achieving salvation.

The Bible teaches the doctrine of total depravity, but that doctrine has been greatly misunderstood. Total depravity does not mean that people have no knowledge of God or righteousness (Rom. 2:14-15), nor that people are as sinful as they can be (2 Tim. 3:13). It does not even mean that people commit every possible type of sin (Mt. 23:23). In fact, some sins rule out other sins. Pride can prevent some individuals from committing other sins. The doctrine of total depravity does not even mean people can never do good works. Most people honor their parents. Even killers don't kill everyone, which is a good thing.

Every Part The doctrine of total depravity means that people lost their holiness in the Fall. They are now unholy, unrighteous, and ungodly (Rom. 5:12, 19; 3:10, 23). Total depravity also means that every part of people was affected by the Fall. Humans now have a darkened mind (2 Cor. 4:4), degraded emotions (Jer. 17:9), and a disobedient will (Rom. 3:11; Isa. 53:6).

Consider Paul's description of unbelievers in Ephesians. "This I say, therefore, and testify in the Lord, that you should no longer walk as the rest of the Gentiles walk, in the futility of their mind, having their understanding darkened, being alienated from the life of God, because of the ignorance that is in them, because of the hardness of their heart; who, being past feeling, have given themselves over to lewdness, to work all uncleanness with greediness" (Eph. 4:17-19). Notice, the references to mind ("the futility of their mind," the "understanding darkened"), emotions ("hardness of their heart," "past feeling") and will ("given themselves," "to work").

The same thing can be seen in Titus. "For we ourselves were also once foolish, disobedient, deceived, serving various lusts and pleasures, living in malice and envy, hateful and hating one another" (Titus 3:3). Again, notice the references to mind ("foolish" means "no understanding"), emotions ("lust and pleasures"), and will ("disobedient," "living in malice").

To say the same thing another way, people react emotionally, think irrationally, act irresponsibly, blame others, and play victim, and if you tell them the truth, they throw stones at you.

Stanley Collins, an English preacher, recounts a childhood incident where he had a half-cent piece, roughly the size of an

American quarter, but needed a whole cent, an English coin equivalent to a half-dollar. A friend suggested that he put it on the rail of a streetcar, which he did. After the train passed over it, the side with the head of the king of England was still there, but the image had been destroyed. Man is like that coin. He had the image of the king impressed and implanted in him, but the Fall destroyed it. Although it can still be faintly seen, it has been destroyed.

A definition of the doctrine of the depravity of people is: When Adam fell, humans lost their holiness, and every part of their personality, including their mind, emotions, and will, was affected.

Summary: Humans were created in the image of God and, thus, have dignity, but because of the Fall, they are depraved. Every part of them has been affected by sin.

If we have the same view of ourselves that God does, we understand that although we have dignity, we are depraved. We will not think too lowly of ourselves, as if we had no worth, nor will we think too highly of ourselves because we are depraved.

If we have the same view of people as the Bible, we will treat people with dignity, even though we know that they are depraved. Children, for example, are to be treated with the utmost dignity and respect, but they are still depraved.

An Englishman with a black hat, gloves, and a cane was walking down the street when he stopped and picked up a penny. Another Englishman who observed his actions said, "I thought you were a gentleman; you picked up a penny!"

"Oh, no!" said the first, "I picked up the image of His majesty." One saw the depravity of humans, the other the dignity of humans. In that people are depraved, it would appear that there is no hope for them. Such is not the case. God goes to work. He does three things to restore His image in people. First, He justifies. When people believe in His Son, God declares them righteous and makes them new creatures with restored, confirmed holiness. That's the point of Ephesians 4:24. Second, God sanctifies. When believers behold His Son in the Word, the Spirit conforms them to God's image (2 Cor. 3:18; Rom. 8:29). Finally, God glorifies. When He raptures believers by His Son, He will make them like His Son (1 Jn. 3:2), who is the image of God (Col. 1:15).

God takes flattened pennies and remakes and restores them.

CHAPTER 11

SIN IS NOT WHAT YOU THINK

In talking to people about the Lord, I have pointed out that the Bible says, "All have sinned" (Rom. 3:23). In the course of the conversation, I ask, "What would you say that means? What is sin?" Answers I have received include, "I am not perfect." "I have made some mistakes." "I'm not what I should or ought to be." "I've broken the Ten Commandments." Answers range from "I dislike myself" to "I have disappointed others" to "I have disobeyed God." What does the Bible say sin is?

The Definition of Sin

What is sin? It may not be what you think it is. Both the Hebrew and Greek words for "sin" mean something like "missing a mark," "overstepping a boundary," etc. In other words, a standard is missed.

What is the standard? Many have said it is the Law of God. For example, the Westminster Larger Catechism declares, "Sin is any want of conformity unto, or transgression of, any law of God." Others have suggested that observation is true, and yet sin is more than that. The standard is not just the Law of God. Romans 3:23 says that all "have sinned and fall short of the glory of God," that is, the divine splendor of God Himself.

That being the case, perhaps a better definition of sin is "Anything contrary to the nature of God." By definition, crime is that which is against the government; sin is that which is against God.

When God wrote the Ten Commandments, He said that the first one is, "You shall have no other gods before Me" (Ex. 20:3). Jesus said, "You shall love the Lord your God with all your heart, with all your soul, with all your mind, and with all your strength" (Mk. 12:30). Unbelievers walk "in the futility of their mind, having their understanding darkened, being alienated from the life of God." (Eph. 4:17-18). These three statements are related to each other. The last one is the most basic description of the spiritual condition of unbelievers. Having been alienated from divine spiritual life, their understanding was darkened, and they lived in futility.

The Different Aspects of Sin

While, in a sense, sin is anything contrary to the nature of God, in another sense, there are different aspects of sin. Theologians say there are four different aspects of sin.

Imputed Sin Romans 5:12 states, "Therefore, just as through one man sin entered the world and death through sin, and thus death spread to all men because all sinned." What does Paul mean when he says that death spread to all because all sinned? Numerous answers have been given.

1. The simplest answer is that it is a reference to personal sin. That is what Paul meant when he used the expression earlier in Romans (Rom. 3:23). According to this view, all died because all sinned. The objection to this explanation is that babies who have not sinned die. Furthermore, in this verse and the rest of the passage, there is a relationship between Adam's sin and the sins of people (Rom. 5:15,

16, 17, 18). Therefore, more than personal sin is involved.
2. The realism view claims the whole human race was present in Adam. They were in him when he sinned (Heb. 7:9-10). All actually sinned in Adam. The objection to this view is that individuals who did not exist cannot act. How can people act before they exist?
3. The imputation explanation teaches that the death of humans results solely from Adam's sin. The Greek word translated "impute" means "to ascribe to, to assign, to change, to credit, to impose." The doctrine of imputed sin is that Adam's sin is imputed to the human race.

While it can be said that there are six different theories of imputation (see Augustus H. Strong, *Systematic Theology*, p. 628), there are only two basic points of view. Some within this group believe in mediate imputation and others believe in immediate imputation.

Mediate imputation is the view that the result of Adam's sin was that all *inherited* a corrupt nature, which is the ground of sin and death. The guilt of the first sin became dependent on the participation in the sin nature. The objection to this position is that the verse does not say all *are* sinners, but all sinned.

Immediate imputation is the theory that Adam was the representative head of the human race, the federal or covenantal representative of all. Therefore, his act was deemed their act; his sin was their sin. Adam's guilt is then immediately (directly) *imputed* to all. The result of the imputation of Adam's sin on the whole human race is guilt and physical death (Rom. 5:12). The objection to the imputation view is that it seems unfair.

As far as that objection is concerned, had those individuals been there, they would have done exactly what Adam did. Besides, there are other imputations in the Scripture, namely, the imputation of the sin of man to Christ and the imputation of the righteousness of Christ to all who trust Christ for eternal life. The truth is that believers benefit from imputation. If it were not for the imputation of sin to Christ and His righteousness to believers, no one would ever be saved.

That kind of thing happens all the time. What happened in the past affects us in the present. My father was born in Greece. As a young man, he and his brother came to this country. What he did back then had a radical impact on me. Had he not come to this country, I would have been in Europe instead of America and spoken Greek instead of English.

All interpretations of Romans 5:12 have problems. Overall, since this exact phrase was used of personal sin in Romans 3:23, it seems best to understand this verse as a reference to personal sin. Cranfield argues that every other occurrence of the verb "to sin" in Pauline epistles is "clearly to actual sin," and there is nothing in the context to suggest that it is being used here in an unusual sense (C. E. B. Cranfield, *The Epistle to the Romans*, p. 279). Of course, not all agree. One objection is that this verse cannot be speaking about personal sin because babes die. Cranfield answers: "Paul must surely be assumed to be thinking in terms of adults" (Cranfield, p. 279).

At the same time, implied in this verse is at least mediate imputation. The reason death spread to all after Adam and all sin now is because Adam's nature was transmitted to all.

Inherent Sin Ephesians 2:3 says that we were by *nature* the children of wrath. This nature, pollution, and corruption must not be thought of as a substance infused into the human soul, but rather, it is simply the doctrine of depravity. Berkhof says, "Inherent corruption extends to every part of man's nature, to all the faculties and powers of both body and soul" (Berkhof, *Systematic Theology*, p. 247). Remember, humans have a darkened mind, degraded emotions, and a disobedient will. People's problems are not just isolated sins. It is their inherent nature.

This aspect of sin is usually called inherent sin. "Inherent" means "the constitution or essential character of anything." The doctrine of inherent sin is: when Adam sinned, he became an entirely different being, degenerate and depraved. His very nature became corrupt. This sinful nature is the opposite of God's nature. Furthermore, every descendant of Adam *inherited* the Adamic, corrupt, depraved, and sinful nature. A definition of the doctrine of inherent sin is that every descendant of Adam inherited the Adamic, corrupt, depraved, and sinful nature (Eph. 2:3). This is sometimes referred to as original sin.

People are not sinners because they sin. They sin because they are sinners.

Some believe that if we could get people to stop doing sinful things, we would solve their problem, but that's not true because that's not the problem. The problem is people's nature. Simply clipping a tiger's claws will not make him lose his taste for blood. People do not need reformation; they need transformation. Merely picking the apples off an apple tree will not stop it from producing them. Its nature must be changed.

Humans are born with a sinful nature, and they manifest it early, as illustrated in a story called "Why Parents Go Grey."

Relating Doctrine To Daily Life

The boss of a big company needed to call one of his employees about an urgent problem with one of the main computers. He dialed the employee's home phone number and was greeted by a child whispering, "Hello?"

Feeling put out at the inconvenience of talking to a youngster, the boss asked, "Is your Daddy home?" "Yes," whispered the small voice. "May I talk with him?" the man asked. To the boss's surprise, the small voice whispered, "No."

Wanting to talk with an adult, the boss asked, "Is your Mommy there?" "Yes," came the answer. "May I talk with her?" Again, the small voice whispered, "No."

Knowing that it was unlikely a young child would be left home alone, the boss decided to leave a message with the person responsible for watching over the child. "Is anyone there besides you?" the boss asked the child. "Yes," whispered the child, "a policeman." Wondering what a cop would be doing at his employee's home, the boss asked, "May I speak with the policeman?" "No, he's busy," whispered the child.

"Busy doing what?" asked the boss. "Talking to Daddy and Mommy and the fireman," came the whispered answer. Growing concerned and even worried, as he heard what sounded like a helicopter through the earpiece on the phone, the boss asked, "What is that noise?"

"A hello-copter," answered the whispering

voice. "What is going on there?" asked the boss, now alarmed. The child answered in an awed whispering voice, "The search team just landed the hello-copper."

Alarmed, concerned, and slightly frustrated, the boss asked, "Why are they there?" Still whispering, the young voice replied with a muffled giggle: "They're looking for me."

Individual Sin Romans 3:23 says, "All have sinned." The Greek word for sin used in this verse means "to miss the mark." As later explained in this verse, the mark is God's glory. Sin, then, is that which is contrary to God's glory, nature, and law, which is a reflection of His character.

This aspect of sin is individual sins. Either intentionally or unintentionally, all commit sins. Thus, the definition of individual sin is: Every human, either intentionally or unintentionally, commits personal sins, which are things contrary to the law of God (Rom. 3:10).

One theologian, Strong, defines sin as selfishness. There is truth to that. Sin very often has a selfish motive and selfishness is very often sinful, but that is not the idea of sin in the Bible. Sin is more than that. It is that which is contrary to God's character and violates God's law. For example, God says, "Don't steal." Most stealing is motivated by selfishness, but some is not. Suppose a man stole to feed his starving family? That motivation may not be strictly selfish, but the action is disobeying the law and depriving the other person of his property.

Individual sins include lawlessness (1 Jn. 3:4), not doing good, that is, sins of omission (Jas. 4:17), and not believing God concerning some particular issue (Rom. 14:23). Personal sins include thoughts, words, and deeds (Mk. 7:21-23).

The State of Sin In several places, the Scripture speaks of being "under sin" (Rom. 3:9; 11:32; Gal. 3:22). This is a state whereby all are sentenced under sin. Walvoord says, "To be under sin is to be divinely reckoned without merit which might contribute toward salvation" (Chafer and Walvoord, *Major Bible Themes*, p. 180). It is the opposite of being in a state of God's favor. Again, this aspect of sin is contrary to God.

This does not mean that all have committed all sins. It means that regardless of the level of sin people have experienced, they are in a state of sin. Imagine three men in a large city. One is the company president on the top floor of a tall building. The second is a salesman working on the first floor. The third is a sewer worker laboring underground. The three are different. They occupy different levels in space, salary, and society, but all are in the state of, say, California. Likewise, people are different in many respects, but all are in the state of sin.

Summary: Sin is everything contrary to the nature of God.

There are three aspects of it. All partake of Adam's nature; it is inherent in us. All produce their sins; we individually do them. All are in a state of sin. Sin is the lack of conformity to God and His law, either in state, disposition, or acts (Rom. 3:23). Sin is not what you think it is. It's worse! People are contrary to God's character and law in state, ancestry, nature, and acts.

That does not mean that every person indulges in every form of sin or that people cannot do any good for others. It does mean that people are sinners by nature and by choice and that God does not accept any of their so-called goodness.

Sin Is Not What You Think

Sin is not what you think. It's worse! It's not just what we do; it is what we are. It is not just that we have all sinned; it is that we are all sinners. People call it an accident; God calls it an abomination. People say it's a blunder; God says it's blindness. People blame chance; God blames choice. People refer to their infirmity; God refers to people's iniquity. People point to their liberty; God points to their lawlessness. People claim the problem is weakness; God declares it is willfulness.

God is the standard. Sin is not simply a failure to live according to our ability but a failure to live according to God's standard.

Sin is a state: the absence of righteousness and the presence of guilt. Sin is a nature: a nature that is enmity toward God. Sin is a clenched fist and its object is the face of God. Sin is an act: an act that is a violation of the law of God.

Don't use this doctrine to excuse sin. At the same time, don't be wiped out when you do sin. Knowing the doctrine of sin should teach you to expect it (knowing other doctrines should teach you to overcome it). Don't use this doctrine to excuse someone else's sin, but also don't be disappointed or discouraged when someone else sins.

The good news is that the Savior solves sin. Jesus Christ takes care of the problem of sin. People inherit Adam's nature, but when they trust Christ, they receive a new nature and the Holy Spirit whereby they can overcome their sinful nature (Rom. 8:2-4). People intentionally sin, but when they trust Christ, they are forgiven (Eph. 1:7). People are in a state of sin, but when they trust Christ, they are no longer in the state of sin; they are in Christ (Eph. 1:3).

It is impossible to illustrate all these aspects of sin and salvation in one story, but suppose a person had a pet tiger that came from a long line of killer tigers, and this tiger broke out, and its tiger nature broke loose. He destroyed property and damaged people until he was hunted like a criminal by the police. Then, suppose his master found him, paid for the damage done, gave him the nature of a lamb, and changed his state from a hunted criminal to a zoo hero. That's fancy, but God does that for us. That is a fact.

CHAPTER 12

WHAT IS ALL THIS "SALVATION" BUSINESS?

A pastor witnessing to a teenager asked, "Have you been saved?" When the young man said, "Yes," the preacher asked, "Tell me how it happened." The teen told this tale: "When I was a small boy, my father took me fishing. We were in a small boat on a big but calm lake when I decided to move from one end of the boat to the other. As I walked back, I slipped and fell into the water. I panicked and screamed and struggled. My father jumped in and pulled me out. That's how I got saved."

That particular story is apocryphal, but the point is accurate. As an itinerant evangelist, I had people tell me similar stories several times. Many people do not understand salvation—at all!

A man saw a billboard that said, "Jesus Saves," and thought it meant that Jesus was thrifty. By the way, he also thought that a bank sponsored the sign.

Most think that being saved is being saved from danger. Christians believe it means to be saved from damnation. Upon hearing several people talking about being saved, I heard of one frustrated fellow who blurted out, "What is all this salvation business about anyway?" Good question.

The word "saved" or "salvation" in the Bible means "to save, deliver, rescue, or even preserve." It is used to deliverance from danger or death (physical). For example, a storm came up when the disciples were on a ship on the Sea of Galilee. The waves were so high that the Bible says they covered the boat. The disciples woke the sleeping Savior and said, "Save us!" (Mt. 8:23-25), that is, "Save us from damage, or even death."

The word "saved" is also used of deliverance from disease. For example, a woman with an issue of blood for twelve years touched the hem of Jesus' garment and the text says that she said within herself, "I shall be made well." The Greek text says, "I shall be saved." Jesus said to her, "Your faith has made you well." Again, the Greek text says, "Your faith has made you saved," that is, "You have been delivered from this disease" (Mt. 9:20-22).

The word is also used of deliverance from damnation. Jesus said, "He will save His people from their sin" (Mt. 1:21), that is, from the punishment of their sin. Salvation, in this case, includes deliverance from damnation.

Thus, the word "save" is used in the Bible to refer to deliverance from danger, disease, death, or damnation. The deliverance can be either physical or spiritual. This provides an overview of how the words "save" and "salvation" are used in the Bible.

Theologians, however, discuss many topics under the title of salvation, including the nature of the election, the extent of the atonement, the work of the Trinity, and even eternal security. It is not the purpose of this discussion to discuss all of the theological ramifications of salvation or even all of the ramifications of the word "salvation" as it is used in the Bible. The purpose of this study is to discuss spiritual salvation, that is, deliverance from sin. (Deliverance from disease, damage, and death will not be discussed.)

The biblical doctrine of spiritual salvation can be divided into three parts. From the standpoint of believers, salvation is past, present, and future. They have been saved (Titus 3:5), they are being saved (1 Cor. 1:18; 1 Tim. 4:16; Jas. 1:21), and they will be saved (Rom. 13:11; 1 Pet. 1:5; Heb. 9:27-28).

Bishop Westcott, the famous English Greek scholar who lived in the nineteenth century, was riding on a train when a boy asked him, "Are you saved?" The Bishop is reported to have replied, "Do you mean, *esothen* (have been saved), or *sodsomai* (am being saved), or *sothesomai* (shall be saved)?" He explained to the boy the meaning of those three Greek words. Although he may not have been appropriate, he was accurate.

Salvation from the Penalty of Sin

The Great Debate over Salvation The great debate over salvation concerns election and free will. Some passages speak of God's sovereign election (Eph. 1:3-14; Rom. 9:11, 15-24; Acts 13:48), and some passages talk of free will (Mt. 23:37; Jn. 3:18, 5:40; 2 Pet. 3:9). Both are true (Eph. 1:12-13; Rom. 10:9-10; Acts 19:9; 2 Thess. 2:13-14). This doctrine is like the doctrine of the Trinity (there is one God but three persons in the Godhead), the doctrine of Christ (He is 100% God and 100% man), and the doctrine of inspiration (the Scripture was written by God and by human authors).

It is an antinomy. In his book *Evangelism and the Sovereignty of God*, J. I. Packer says a theological antinomy is "an apparent incompatibility between two apparent 'truths.'" He says it is a pair of principles that are "seemingly irreconcilable, yet both are undeniable" (Packer, p. 18). This is in contrast to a paradox, which is merely a verbal contradiction (Packer, p. 20). Packer insists that God's sovereignty and man's responsibility are taught side by side and sometimes in the same text (Lk. 22:22; Acts 2:23).

The Terms Used for Salvation The Bible teaches that all have sinned and the penalty of sin is death. Salvation is deliverance from the penalty of sin. Believers *have been* saved (Titus 3:5). This is phase one of a believer's salvation. The Scripture employs several distinct terms to describe this phase of salvation.

1. Forgiveness. The Greek word "forgive" means "to send away." God takes away our sins and sends them away because of the death of Christ. His death paid the penalty for sin so God can forgive (Col. 1:14).

2. Regeneration. Another term used for this phase of salvation is regeneration (Titus 3:5). This doctrine was discussed in the chapter on the Holy Spirit.

3. Justification. The Bible also uses the word justification to refer to this aspect of salvation (Titus 3:7; Rom. 3:24). "To justify" means "to declare righteous." It does not mean to *make* righteous but to *declare* righteous. It is a legal term that refers to the verdict of a court. The doctrine of justification is defined as the moment when people place their faith in Jesus Christ, God declaring them righteous (Rom. 3:24).

Suppose a man were charged with the crime of robbery. A clerk swore that he was the man who held him up. The man's defense was that he didn't do it. Maybe someone who looked like him did, but it was not him. During the trial, the prosecuting attorney dogmatically declared the man was guilty. The clerk testified. Then, the defense attorney presented his case. He said, "This man cannot be guilty because, on the night in question, he was preaching before a congregation of people, hundreds of whom will parade before this court and testify that at the time of the crime, he was standing before them speaking." In such a case, the jury would justify the charged man, that is, pronounce him innocent, not guilty, righteous as far as that crime was concerned. How can God pronounce a sinner righteous when the sinner is guilty before Him? The answer is that Christ died and paid the penalty for sin. Based on that, God can forgive and declare the sinner righteous (Rom. 3:24; 2 Cor. 5:21).

Romans 4:3-5 states that Abraham's belief in God was counted to him for righteousness. The word "counted" is an accounting term that means "reckon to my account." When people pay their bills, the payment is credited to their account. Likewise, Christ paid and God credited His payment and His righteousness to the account of sinners. Thus, sinners are saved, that is, delivered, from the penalty and punishment of their sin.

Although justification and regeneration happen at the moment of conversion, they are different. Justification has to do with people's standing before God. They are unrighteous but declared righteous. Regeneration has to do with people's state before God. They were dead; now they are alive to God. Justification is objective; regeneration is subjective.

The Basis of Salvation The basis of salvation is the death and resurrection of Jesus Christ, which is the essence of the gospel. First Corinthians 15:1-8 is the only passage in the New Testament that defines the gospel. Paul begins by telling the Corinthians that he is about to declare to them the gospel, that is, the good news, by which they were saved (1 Cor. 15:1-2). Then, in 1 Corinthians 15:3-5, he defines the gospel.

Paul states four things about Christ: 1) He died for our sins, 2) He was buried, 3) He arose, and 4) He was seen. Concerning two of these items, he says, "according to the Scripture," thus indicating that the two basic elements of the gospel are: Christ died for our sins and Christ rose from the dead. Christ's burial is proof of His death, and His appearances are proof of His resurrection.

A definition of the gospel is: The gospel is the good news that Jesus Christ died for our sins and bodily rose from the dead (1 Cor. 15:1-8). It is the gospel "by which also you are saved" (1 Cor. 15:2).

The Means of Salvation The means of salvation are repentance and faith. The Greek word "repent," which occurs fifty-eight times in the New Testament, basically means "to change one's mind." It describes an inward change of thinking or attitude (*cf.* "repent" in Acts 8:22 with "you thought" in Acts 8:20 and " your heart" in Acts 8:21, etc.). It is not being sorry for sin (2 Cor. 7:9, where being sorry and repentance are clearly two different things), nor is it turning from sin (Acts 26:20, which literally says, "Repent *and* turn to God," indicating that repentance and turning are two distinct things).

The objects of repentance vary. Sometimes, God is the object (Acts 20:21), but at other times dead works are said to be the object (Heb. 6:1; Rev. 9:20; 16:11; etc.). The object of repentance mentioned in Acts 2:38 is Christ. Sin is also, on occasion, the object of repentance (Rev. 9:21). The context must determine the object of the person's change of mind.

Thus, the definition of repentance is a change of mind concerning God, Christ, works, and sin (Acts 17:30).

The Greek word "faith," which in both its noun and verb forms occurs 492 times in the New Testament, means "to accept something as true and depend on it." Faith assumes that the person has information to accept as true, etc. Therefore, many have pointed out that the three elements of faith are knowledge, mental assent, and trust. In the case of salvation, faith is believing that Jesus Christ is the Son of God (Jn. 20:31), God in the flesh

(1 Jn. 4:2), who died for sin (Rom. 3:25), and rose from the dead (Rom. 10:9).

Thus, the definition of faith in salvation from the penalty of sin is the belief that Jesus Christ, the God/Man, died for my sin and rose from the dead, and trust in Him for the gift of eternal life (1 Tim. 1:16).

Repentance and faith are not two steps in salvation; they are one. When repentance appears alone in the New Testament as the requirement of salvation, it must include faith. When faith is listed as the only requirement, it of necessity includes repentance. Therefore, while repentance and faith are not synonymous, they are inseparable. They cannot be separated, but they can be distinguished (Acts 20:21).

Imagine a boy in a boat who falls into a lake and is rescued. That's not a bad illustration of salvation. The lake is sin, and we are all drowning in it. The Lord dives in and saves us. Phase one is pulling us from the water.

Salvation from the Power of Sin

Believers in Jesus Christ have been saved. That is a past, completed act. Yet, the Bible teaches that they are also in the process of being saved, which is a present, continuous action whereby they are saved from the power of sin (1 Cor. 1:18).

The Flesh This aspect of salvation is desperately needed in the lives of believers because even though they have been forgiven—declared righteous, and have a new nature—they still can sin. This capacity to sin is called "the flesh" (Gal. 5:19-21). Thus, people can be saved and still sin. They can be saved, but they still need to be saved. They can be saved from the penalty of sin, but they also need saving from the power of sin.

The Corinthians were saved; they were called saints (1 Cor. 1:2) and even righteous (1 Cor. 1:30). Yet there were many sins in their midst, including divisions (1 Cor. 1-4), sexual sins, including incest (1 Cor. 5) and using prostitutes (1 Cor. 6). They were taking each other to court (1 Cor. 6); they had doctrinal problems with tongues, and some even denied the resurrection (1 Cor. 15:12). These Corinthians were saved, but they needed saving from sin, self, and the severe punishment of God (1 Cor. 11:30).

The Word What is the solution to this? James says, "The Word is able to save your soul" (Jas. 1:21), literally translated "save your life." Obedience to the Word of God will keep believers from wasting their lives in the world.

The Holy Spirit Paul adds that walking in the Spirit will prevent a believer from fulfilling the desires of the flesh (Gal. 5:16). As believers know the Word and walk in it by dependence on the Holy Spirit, they will be saved from the power of sin.

Remember the boy drowning in the lake being rescued? That was phase one. Phase two is the Lord on the beach, instructing us how not to be overcome by water again.

The flesh dictates, "Be bitter and hate." The power of the flesh pulls the believer into sin. The Word says, "Love," and the Spirit of God gives the believer the power to exercise love. So, as believers choose to love and depend upon God for the grace to do it, they are saved from hate and its consequences.

Salvation from the Presence of Sin

As was pointed out earlier, there is a future salvation. This phase of salvation is deliverance from the very presence of sin (Rom. 13:11; Heb. 9:28; 1 Pet. 1:5).

The World The world is filled with sin, from A to Z: adultery, bitterness, covetousness, drunkenness, envy, fornication, griping, hatred, idolatry, jealousy, killing, lying, mugging, murder, nakedness, orgies, pride, quarreling, reveling, strife, theft, thievery, unthankfulness, variance, witchcraft, X-rated movies, yelling and the zodiac.

Deliverance In John 14, Jesus informed the disciples that He was preparing a place for believers and that He would one day return to get them and take them there. That's heaven, away from this sin-saturated society. Believers need to be delivered from the very presence of sin.

When Christ returns and receives believers unto Himself, they will be delivered from the presence of those sins and the self inside themselves. Paul says our bodies will be like unto His body (Phil. 3:21). John says we will be like Him, for we shall see Him as He is (1 Jn. 3:2). The Christian needs to be delivered, not only from the sin outside but also the sin from within. Deliverance from the presence of sin includes both.

Remember the illustration of the boy being rescued from drowning? Phase one was being rescued from the water. Phase two is being instructed on the shore. Well, phase three is being flown away from the lake in a helicopter from the very presence of the water.

Summary: Spiritual salvation is deliverance from sin, its penalty, power, and presence.

A definition of the doctrine of salvation is: God saves individuals from the penalty of sin when they trust His Son, Jesus Christ; He is in the process of delivering them from the power of sin in this life and will ultimately deliver them from the very presence of sin (Eph. 2:8; Jas. 1:21; 1 Pet. 1:5). To be delivered (saved) from the penalty of sin, one must trust Christ. To be delivered from the power of sin, believers must obey Christ. The question is, "Are you saved and are you being saved?"

I was with a small group of believers discussing salvation when a new lady began to make statements, indicating to everyone present that she was somewhat confused about the subject. Several in the group tried to clear up the confusion, but the lady didn't understand. As I listened to the exchange, I crafted an illustration that cleared up the confusion. Here is what I told her.

Imagine that Hawaii is heaven, you are in the continental US, and you want to get there. If you tried to swim there, you would not make it. You may swim further than some others and some might swim further than you, but all would fall short of the Hawaiian shore. Suppose in your attempt, you began to drown when a cruise liner going to Hawaii came along and rescued you. That is a picture of phase one salvation.

Once onboard, out of gratitude, you could be as kind and helpful. Or you could be your selfish self. If you were being your same old self, you would need to be rescued again. That illustrates phase two of salvation: being rescued on the way to heaven.

Phase three is making it to Hawaii.

CHAPTER 13

PLEASE EXPLAIN SANCTIFICATION

As a young Christian, I wanted to scream, "Will somebody please explain sanctification to me?" As a non-Christian, "sanctification" was not in my vocabulary. Then, when I became a Christian, I found that no two Christians seemed to agree on what it meant.

Most Christians who used the word said it meant a second work of grace whereby God made you holy. According to them, you needed to "pray through," that is, hang on to God until He blesses you this second and final time.

Other Christians didn't use the word much, but when they did, they disagreed with those who used it all the time. This bunch seemed to feel that rather than "hanging on," you needed to "let go and let God."

I was confused. Was I to let go or hang on? To add to the muddle in my mind, the pastors and preachers I respected the most never used the word at all!

I finally decided that if you were sanctified (however you got it), it meant that you didn't do the "filthy five:" drink, smoke, go to movies, dance, or play cards. What I really wanted was for someone to "please explain sanctification to me."

The Word The Greek word translated "sanctify" means "to separate, to set apart, to make holy." In the Bible, it is applied to God, things, people, and places. God is holy, set apart from His creatures called humans and from corruption called sin

(Lev. 11:44). The third person of the Trinity is called the *Holy Spirit*. Things and people are set apart; for example, the Tabernacle was sanctified (Ex. 29:44) and so were the priests (Ex. 29:44). The basic concept is to set apart.

Wives have all kinds of pots, pans, and containers in their kitchens. Those utensils are sanctified. They have been set apart for cooking. Consequently, they stay in the kitchen under her care and for her use. Suppose a husband needed a container for gas or oil and went into the kitchen and took one of his wife's pots. If she caught him in the act, she would surely inquire, "What are you going to do with my pot?" If he explained that he was about to put something such as gas or oil in it, she might inform him, "That pot is sanctified!" Just as a wife's kitchen pots are separated from gas and oil, and for food, and from her husband to her, so believers are separated from sin and to God.

Biblical Usage Theologians use the word "sanctification" to refer to justification, sanctification, and glorification. In other words, there are three aspects of sanctification.

Positional Sanctification

According to the New Testament, believers have been set apart to God. That is their position. The writer to the Hebrews says, "We have been sanctified through the offering of the body of Jesus Christ once for all" (Heb. 10:10).

Positional sanctification is defined as the work of God, whereby He sets believers apart to Himself to be saints. This aspect of sanctification is popularly and correctly called being born again or being saved. Contrary to popular impression, in the Bible, it is also called sanctification (Heb. 10:10).

The Death of Christ The death of Christ accomplishes positional sanctification. By the shedding of His blood, He paid for sin and bought us for Himself, thus setting us apart (Heb. 10:10). The doctrine of redemption is that God bought us and set us free. The concept in this aspect of sanctification is that He bought us and set us apart for Himself. It's like saying that a wealthy man went to the slave market, bought a slave, and made him his son.

The Work of the Holy Spirit This aspect of sanctification is also accomplished by the Holy Spirit (2 Thess. 2:13; 1 Pet. 1:2; Rom. 15:16). The Holy Spirit sets us apart to God through the process of convicting us of sin, enlightening us concerning the gospel of the grace of God, and drawing us to a point where we place our trust in Christ.

Faith Phase one of our sanctification is accomplished by faith (2 Thess. 2:12-13). The Holy Spirit works, yet the individual must trust in Jesus Christ. People who trust Jesus Christ for eternal life are positionally sanctified and set apart unto God. To say the same thing another way, they are saints (1 Cor. 1:2).

In some branches of Christianity, people are canonized after they die. The New Testament teaches that believers are canonized while they are alive, the moment they trust Christ. Positional sanctification is as complete for the weakest saint as it is for the most mature.

Let me illustrate. There is something at your house that is sanctified. It has been set apart by you for you. It is personal to you. It didn't cost much, and you don't pay much attention to it. You alone use it. No one else would even think of using it, not even a close friend, or, for that matter, your mother, and if they did use it even once, you would probably never use it again. Others may watch you use yours. They may use their own, but they don't use yours. You use it every day, I hope. I am speaking of your toothbrush. You have set it apart for your personal use. Likewise, believers have been set apart (sanctified) for God's personal use.

Progressive Sanctification

The second aspect of sanctification is called progressive sanctification. Paul says, "Now may the God of peace Himself sanctify you completely; and may your whole spirit, soul, and body be preserved blameless at the coming of our Lord Jesus Christ" (1 Thess. 5:23).

Progressive sanctification is defined as the work of God, whereby we are practically and progressively set apart to be saintly. The Shorter Catechism says, "It is the work of God's free grace, whereby we are renewed in the whole man after the image of God and are enabled more and more to die unto sin and to live unto righteousness" (1 Cor. 4:3; 5:23; 2 Cor. 7:1).

It is this phase of sanctification that is commonly referred to as sanctification. It is an aspect of sanctification that is distinct from justification. Justification is the act of God whereby He declares the sinner righteous. Sanctification is the work of God whereby He works in the saint the righteousness He declared at justification. In justification, believers are declared righteous so that they may become righteous in sanctification. The first is an act; the second is a process. Justification is what God does *for* us. Sanctification is what God does *in* us.

Justification and sanctification are, in a sense, paradoxical. Justification proclaims believers are already clean. Sanctification commands them to cleanse themselves. Justification declares believers righteous. Sanctification demands that they be righteous.

Justification says they are complete. Sanctification says they still have a lack. One is their position; the other is their practice. Believers need to become what they are.

Perhaps one of the most critical comparisons that can be made between justification and sanctification is this: justification is by faith alone; sanctification involves both faith and effort. That brings up the process of progressive sanctification.

The Word of God Progressive sanctification is accomplished by the Word of God (Jn. 17:17). How does the Word of God sanctify? William Evans has said, "By revealing sins; by awakening conscience; by revealing the character of Christ; by showing the example of Christ; by affecting the influences and power of the Holy Spirit; and by setting forth spiritual motives and ideals" (Evans, *Great Doctrines of the Bible*, p. 169).

Faith and Obedience Progressive sanctification is also accomplished by faith (Rom. 1:17; Gal. 2:20; Heb. 10:38) and obedience (Rom. 6:16, 19, 22), as well as chastening (Heb. 12:9-11). Sinners cannot put forth effort or do any work that will make them saints. They can only simply and solely trust in Jesus Christ. God then places them in the position of being saints, but not all saints act like saints. For saints to become saintly, they must have their minds renewed by the Word of God and they must believe and obey what that Word says. Believers will never experience progressive sanctification by passive surrender alone. There must be active obedience (2 Tim. 2:21; 1 Tim. 4:7).

Let me illustrate the concept of progressive sanctification. Carol Talbot, the wife of Dr. Louis T. Talbot, tells of finding her toothbrush one morning on the floor of the bathtub. She asked her husband how her toothbrush landed in the bathtub. He calmly replied that he was scrubbing his corns with it. He also confessed (remember that Dr. Talbot was a great practical joker) that he had used it to brush his hair and scrub his fingernails. His wife asked, "If you must use a toothbrush for all that, why don't you use your own?" He meekly admitted he could never find it. So, she bought him a whole glassful of toothbrushes and hid her own.

The point is that Carol Talbot's toothbrush was bought, set apart, and used exclusively by her. It was positionally sanctified, but if, in truth, her husband was using it to scrub his corns, it was not progressively being sanctified.

Prospective Sanctification

The third aspect of sanctification is prospective sanctification. Prospective sanctification is the work of God whereby we are finally and wholly set apart unto Him (1 Thess. 4:17). This aspect of sanctification will be accomplished by the Rapture when the Lord catches up all believers to be with Himself. Then they shall be like Him (1 Jn. 3:2) and will be forever with Him (1 Thess. 4:17). That will be complete sanctification: set apart, separated, like Him and with Him.

Mrs. Talbot's toothbrush was positionally sanctified the day she bought it. Then she discovered she was having trouble keeping it set apart for her own exclusive use. The only way she could keep her toothbrush wholly set apart for her use would be to keep it with her all the time. Similarly, there will come a day when God will wholly sanctify all believers by keeping them with Himself all the time.

Summary: Sanctification means "to set apart." The spiritual sanctification of people is the work of God, whereby He sets them apart to Himself. He does this in three stages: positionally by the blood of Christ, progressively by the Word of Christ, and prospectively by the coming of Christ.

A definition of the doctrine of sanctification is the work of God whereby He positionally, progressively, and ultimately sets believers apart to Himself (2 Thess. 2:13; Jn. 17:17; 1 Thess. 4:17).

Sanctification, then, is not sanctimoniousness, a second blessing, or the eradication of sinful nature. Some people want to turn sanctification into a list of taboos, such as not wearing makeup. Frankly, God is not as interested in what goes on the lips as what comes through them.

Practical sanctification is not instantaneous; it is the progressive work of God in the life of the believer. It is not without effort, nor is it passive; it requires great effort and discipline on the believer's part. It is not yet, nor will it be in this life, complete; it is progressive. It is not just external; it begins and is very much involved with internal aspects.

Only with great effort will believers progressively become holy and, even then, never completely so in this life. God has made them positionally holy and will one day make them completely holy. In the meantime, God wants believers to strive toward holiness and never be satisfied with whatever level they obtain.

It is like a pole-vaulter. He works to make a mark and when he has made it, he moves it higher. He is never satisfied. God's will is for believers to keep perfecting holiness and never be satisfied with any level of holiness they should attain in this life.

CHAPTER 14

WHAT IS THE CHURCH?

"A child of seven years knows what the church is," Martin Luther once wrote: "It is made up of holy believers and lambs who hear the voice of the Good Shepherd." I wonder if Martin Luther would say that today. Today, most seven-year-olds, seventeen-year-olds, or twenty-seven-year-olds do not know what the church is.

When most people hear the word "church," they immediately think of a building. The type of building depends on the area of the country in which one grew up. A New Englander thinks of a white wooden-frame church with a steeple on top. Southerners imagine a red brick Colonial-style church with a steeple on top and four white columns in the front. Someone from an inner-city ghetto remembers a storefront.

In Omaha, Nebraska, a store named Kum & Go applied for a liquor license. The city denied the license because it was within 150 feet of the House of Faith. The store then obtained a license from the state Liquor Control Commission, claiming the House of Faith didn't meet the criteria for a church. The commission said a church is "a building owned by a religious organization used primarily for religious purposes." In other words, according to them, a church has to own a building to be a church. The last I heard, the Nebraska Supreme Court was being asked to define a church! (*Los Angeles Times*, April 6, 2002).

When some hear the word "church," they might think of a denomination like Roman Catholic, Lutheran, Presbyterian,

Episcopalian, Baptist, Methodist, or Pentecostal. What, then, is the church? How is the word used in the Bible, and what does it mean?

The Greek word translated "church" means "assembly." The Bible uses it in a secular and spiritual sense. In the secular sense, it refers to a town meeting (Acts 19:39, 41). In the spiritual sense, it refers to the universal church and local churches.

The Universal Church

Definition To understand the concept of the universal church, several passages of Scripture must be put together. The first is in 1 Corinthians: "For by one Spirit we were all baptized into one body; whether Jews or Greeks, whether slaves or free; and have all been made to drink into one Spirit" (1 Cor. 12:13). Notice the word "all." When all trust Christ for eternal life, they are immediately baptized into one body. The body into which all are baptized is the body of Christ. Paul says God "put all things under His (Christ's) feet, and gave Him to be head over all things to the church, which is His body, the fullness of Him who fills all in all" (Eph. 1:22-23). The body of Christ is the church. In other words, when people trust Christ, they are placed into the body of Christ, which is the church. Since *all* believers are members of this church, it is called the universal church.

All who trust in Christ are related to one another. When I meet another believer anywhere in the world, I feel an immediate connection. We are both members of the same body, the same church.

The Beginning When did the church begin? Throughout church history, especially the last four or five hundred years, there has been much discussion and debate about when the church began. Covenant theologians tend to place the church in the Old Testament, with some extending its roots as far back as Abraham or Adam. Dispensationalists have traditionally taught that the church began on the day of Pentecost. Ultra-dispensationalists contend that the church began after Pentecost, some pushing it as late as after the close of the book of Acts.

The word "church" does not occur in the Old Testament in the sense of the universal church of Christ. It only occurs three times in all of the Gospels, and in one of those references, it is apparent that it is still in the future (Mt. 16:18).

Since the universal church is the spiritual baptism of believers into the body of Christ, the answer to the question of when the church began is the answer to the question of when the baptism of the Holy Spirit began.

The baptism of the Holy Spirit, which places people into the body of Christ, the church, began on Pentecost. Acts 1:5 states, "For John truly baptized with water, but you shall be baptized with the Holy Spirit not many days from now." Obviously, at that point, the baptism of the Holy Spirit was still in the future.

Acts 2 records that the Holy Spirit descended on 120 believers on the day of the Feast of Pentecost. It says nothing about the baptism of the Holy Spirit. In Acts 10, while Peter was preaching to Cornelius and his household, the Holy Spirit fell on all of those who heard the Word (Acts 10:44-47). When Peter returned to Jerusalem to explain what happened at Caesarea, he said, "And as I began to speak, the Holy Spirit fell upon them as upon us at the beginning. Then I remembered the word of the Lord how He said, 'John, indeed, baptized with water, but you shall be baptized with the Holy Spirit'" (Acts 11:15-16).

Notice carefully that Peter calls what happened in Acts 10, the baptism of the Holy Spirit and says that it was the same thing that happened to "us at the beginning." In Acts 1:5, the baptism of the Holy Spirit was still in the future. The expression "at the beginning" then must be a reference to Acts 2. Therefore, the baptism of the Holy Spirit began on the day of Pentecost as recorded in Acts 2.

Since the baptism of the Holy Spirit is that act of Christ and the Holy Spirit that places believers into the body of Christ, which is the church, and it began on the day of Pentecost, it is clear that the church began on the day of Pentecost.

The Disappearance At the Rapture, the church will be taken out to be with Christ. The word "church" never occurs after Revelation 3, but more about that in the chapter on prophecy. The universal church, then, consists of people saved from Pentecost until the Rapture. The area of Scripture that deals with the church begins in the book of Acts and goes through Revelation 3.

At any rate, a definition of the universal church doctrine is the spiritual organism composed of all people who have been saved from Pentecost to the Rapture (Mt. 16:18). Obviously, that assembly has never been assembled.

The Local Church

When the New Testament uses the word "church," it usually refers to a local church. What is a local church? Is it a building with a steeple, stained glass, and a pulpit? In the biblical sense, the answer is "No." As we have seen, the Greek word literally means "assembly." The church is not a building; it is an assembly of people.

What Is The Church?

There is a great deal of fuzzy, out-of-focus thinking on the part of American Christians concerning the church because of the popular meaning of the English word church. American Christians use the word church to refer to a building. It is common to hear someone say, "Their church has 3,000 seats," but their church cannot have 3,000 seats. It cannot have any seats. In the biblical sense of the term, the church is made up of people. Their church may meet in a building that has 3,000 seats.

On the other hand, an assembly of people who are Christians is not necessarily a church either. Believers could meet in a football stadium for an evangelistic meeting, but that would not make them a local church.

When the word "church" is used in the New Testament to refer to a local church, it refers to a group of believers who are baptized and organized for a specific purpose. So, a simple definition of the local church is a group of baptized believers organized to do God's work and will. The organizational structure of a local church is at least outlined in the New Testament. The ordinances and orders of the church are also specifically given.

Organization Five statements spell out, as well as summarize, the organization of the church in the New Testament: Christ is the Head of the Church. Elders are responsible for the Church. Deacons serve. Gifted believers equip the saints. All believers minister.

Christ is the Head of the church (Eph. 1:22-23), not the congregation nor the official board. When any group within the church or when the whole church meets together, the issue is not what *I* want but what *His* will is.

Elders are responsible for seeing that God's will is carried out in a church. Each congregation should have a plurality of elders.

That is obvious from the fact that the New Testament says that there are elders (plural) in every church (singular) (Acts 14:23; 20:17; Jas. 5:14). The qualifications for elders are given in 1 Timothy 3:1-7 and Titus 1:5-9. This group of elders is responsible for seeing to it that the flock is fed (Acts 20:28; 1 Pet. 5:2), exhorted (Titus 1:9) and, if necessary, rebuked (Titus 1:9). They're also in charge of finances (Acts 11:30). In short, elders rule (1 Tim. 5:18). Therefore, members are exhorted to obey those who have the rule over them (Heb. 13:7, 17; 1 Thess. 5:12).

This does not mean that elders are to be dictators. Peter says elders are not to lord it over the flock (1 Pet. 5:3), but neither should a congregation demand a democracy.

Deacons are to serve. The Greek word translated "deacon" means "servant." The qualifications for deacons are given in 1 Tim. 3:8-13. Beyond that, very little is said about deacons. Some say that Acts 6:1-7 refers to deacons, but that is conjecture. The New Testament nowhere indicates that they are to meet as a board, make decisions, or even care for money. They are to serve, probably in carrying out the decisions of the elders. Certainly, they are under the supervision of the elders.

Gifted believers are to equip the saints. In Ephesians 4, Paul states that God gives gifts to believers and places those gifted individuals within the church (Eph. 4:7-16). These gifted believers are to equip the saints (Eph. 4:12). They are not necessarily to rule. Instead, they are to minister with the Word (1 Pet. 4:11). These are those with a speaking gift, such as teaching, evangelizing, exhorting, etc.

All believers are to minister. Throughout the epistles of the New Testament, believers are constantly exhorted to minister to one another. Christians are not to attend church to be spectators but to participate (Heb. 10:25).

I wear three hats in my church. I am an elder, a gifted believer, and a member. As an elder, I meet with the other elders and we make decisions, such as who should be accepted into the membership of this local church. As a believer with the gift of pastor/teacher, I equip other believers by teaching the Word of God. I am also a member. As a member, I give money and minister to people on a one-to-one basis.

Ordinances The church, as an organized group of baptized believers, meets to carry out God's Word. Part of the will of God for the church is that they regularly observe two ordinances: baptism and the Lord's Supper.

Baptism is one of the battlegrounds of basic Bible doctrine. For centuries, Christians have debated and been divided over the meaning, matter, and mode of baptism. What is the meaning of baptism? That is, what does it do? Is it a symbol, or is it a requirement for salvation? And who is its subject? Is it for babies or believers? What about its mode? How is it to be done? Are people to be dipped in water, or will a few drops be dropped on their heads?

Baptism is a symbol (1 Pet. 3:21) of union with Christ (Rom. 6:3-5) and His body (1 Cor. 12:13). It does not save, which is evident from the fact that in Acts 10, people received the Holy Spirit before they were baptized (Acts 10:44-47).

Baptism is for believers, not babies (Acts 18:8). There is not one clear-cut case of baby baptism in the entire Bible. If infant baptism is as important as those who practice it say it is, why did God not give one clear case of it in the Bible?

Baptism is to be by immersion. The word "baptism" means "to dip or immerse." John the Baptist baptized "in Aenon near

Salim because there was much water there" (Jn. 3:23). Ryrie says, "The first exception to immersion was pouring, not sprinkling, and it was allowed in cases that could not be immersed, such as sick people. Indeed, pouring was called 'clinic' baptism. Cyprian (AD 200-257) was evidently the first to approve of sprinkling, though it was not generally practiced until the 12th century" (Ryrie, *A Survey of Bible Doctrine*, p. 152).

The Lord's Supper is another battleground. The war rages over its meaning. Is it a sacrament, a means of grace, or a symbol?

The Roman Catholic Church teaches the doctrine of transubstantiation, that is, that the bread and wine become the actual body and blood of Christ. Lutherans believe in consubstantiation. In their view, there is no change in the elements, but somehow, Christ is "in, with, and under" the bread and the wine. Most Protestants contend that the Lord's Supper is merely a memorial, a symbolic remembrance of Christ's death.

Those who believe that the Lord's Supper is a sacrament point to the fact that Jesus said, "This is My body ... blood" (Mt. 26:26-28), and insist that "is" means "is." Those holding to the symbolic viewpoint of the verse where Jesus said, "This do in remembrance of Me" (Lk. 22:19). Who is right?

The Bible supports the symbolic position. In the Scripture, "is" can be figurative as well as literal. Jesus said, "I am the door" ("am," a form of "is," is figuratively used in that sentence). Furthermore, when He said, "This *is* My blood," it was figurative, for at that time, His literal blood was still in His veins.

The definition of an ordinance is an outward symbol of a spiritual truth commanded by Christ to be performed by the church. There are two ordinances: baptism (Mt. 28:19) and the Lord's Table (1 Cor. 11:23-32). The two ordinances of the church are both symbolic, but just because they are symbolic does not mean that they should be treated lightly. The flag is a symbol, but citizens treat it with respect because of what it represents.

A man carries a picture of his wife as a symbol to help him remember her. There are two extremes to which a man could go with such a picture. One would be to treat it as if it were the real thing. Or, he could never look at it or even throw darts at it. Neither extreme makes much sense.

Orders The third aspect of the local church is its orders. After the resurrection of Christ and before His ascension, He repeatedly appeared to the apostles. On several of these occasions, He gave them what is commonly called the Great Commission. Five forms of it are recorded in the New Testament (Mt. 28:16-20; Mk. 16:14-18; Lk. 24:44-49; Jn. 20:19-23; Acts 1:6-11). An examination of the five passages containing the Great Commission reveals that the overriding overall commission is to make disciples. To make disciples, the church must be involved in evangelism, winning people to Jesus Christ, and education, teaching believers the Word of God. (For a more detailed explanation of these passages, see G. Michael Cocoris, *Evangelism: A Biblical Approach*.) The process also includes other things like baptism, observance of the Lord's Table, prayers, fellowship, etc. (Acts 2:41, 42).

Churches today are like doctors; they want to specialize. So, some are specialists in evangelism. Others are surgeons of Christian Education. A new breed is an expert on edification. However, God has commanded the church to be a general practitioner. Each local church must be involved in all of these areas.

Thus, the local church is defined as a group of baptized believers organized to do God's work and will (Acts 14:23).

Summary: The essence of the biblical doctrine of the church is that there is a universal church, which is a spiritual organism composed of all saved people in this dispensation, which, in turn, manifests itself in local churches, which are organized groups of baptized believers.

If there is a common idea between these two elements, it is the concept of "assembly." Hebrews 10:25 talks about local churches when it speaks of assembling ourselves together. Second Thessalonians 2:1 has in mind the universal church and speaks of our gathering together to Him. In the Greek text, both verses use the same phrase translated in one, "assembling ourselves," and in the other, "gathering together." Believers assemble together here in various locations; one day, all believers will be assembled there. What a meeting that will be!

Your relationship and responsibility to your local church can be summarized in three practical suggestions: 1) Attend it—Hebrews 10:25. 2) Support it—Galatians 6:6-9. 3) Minister to others while there—Hebrews 10:24-25.

What kind of church member are you? Someone has said there are four types: those who are tired, they're always too tired to do anything; those who are tiresome, they render service but do so grudgingly; those who are retired, they used to work, but they quit; and then there are those who are tireless, they work, enjoy it, and never seem to tire.

What if?

It's a Wednesday night and you are at a church prayer meeting when somebody runs in from the parking lot and says, "Turn on a radio, turn on a radio."

While the church listens to a small radio, the announcement is made: "Two women are lying in a Long Island hospital, dying from the mystery flu." Within hours, it swept across the country. People are working around the clock, trying to find an antidote.

Nothing is working in California, Oregon, Arizona, Florida, and Massachusetts. It's as though it's just sweeping in from the borders. And then, all of a sudden, the news comes out. The code has been broken. A cure can be found. A vaccine can be made. It's going to take the blood of somebody who hasn't been infected, and so, sure enough, all through the Midwest, through all those channels of emergency broadcasting, everyone is asked to do one simple thing: Go to your downtown hospital and have your blood type taken. That's all we ask of you.

When you hear the sirens go off in your neighborhood, please make your way quickly, quietly, and safely to the hospital. Sure enough, when you and your family get down there late on that Friday night, there is a long line, and they've got nurses and doctors coming out and pricking fingers and taking blood and putting labels on it.

Your wife and kids are out there, and they take your blood type. They say, "Wait here in the parking lot, and if we call your name, you can be dismissed and go home."

You stand around, scared, with your neighbors, wondering what's happening in the world and if this is the end of the world.

Suddenly, a young man comes running out of the hospital screaming. He's yelling a name and waving a clipboard.

What? He yells it again! And your son tugs on your jacket and says, "Daddy, that's me." Before you know it, they have grabbed your boy. Wait a minute. Hold on!

And they say, "It's okay, his blood is clean. His blood is pure.

We want to make sure he doesn't have the disease. We think he has got the right type."

Five tense minutes later, the doctors and nurses come out, crying and hugging one another—some are even laughing. It's the first time you have seen anybody laugh in a week, and an old doctor walks up to you and says, "Thank you, sir. Your son's blood type is perfect. It's clean and pure, and we can make the vaccine." As the word begins to spread across that parking lot full of folks, people are screaming, praying, laughing, and crying.

Then the gray-haired doctor pulls you and your wife aside and says, "May we see you for a moment? We didn't realize that the donor would be a minor and we need you to sign a consent form."

You begin to sign, only to see that the line for the number of pints of blood to be taken is blank. So you ask, "How many pints?"

And that is when the old doctor's smile fades and he says, "We had no idea it would be a little child. We weren't prepared. We need it all."

"But, but ...You don't understand."

"We are talking about the world here. Please sign. We need it all!"

"But can't you give him a transfusion?"

"If we had clean blood, we would. Can you sign? Would you sign?" In numb silence, you do.

Then they say, "Would you like to have a moment with him before we begin?"

Can you walk back? Can you walk back to that room where he sits on a table, saying, "Daddy? Mommy? What's going on?" Can you take his hands and say, "Son, your mommy and I love you, and we would never ever let anything happen to you that didn't just have to be. Do you understand that?"

When that old doctor comes back in, he says, "I'm sorry, we've got to get started. People all over the world are dying. Can you leave? Can you walk out while he is saying, "Dad? Mom? Dad? Why, why have you forsaken me?"

When they have the ceremony to honor your son, some folks sleep through it, some don't even come because they go to the lake, and some come with a pretentious smile and just pretend to care. You would want to jump up and say, "MY SON DIED FOR YOU! DON'T YOU CARE?"

Is that what GOD wants to say? "MY SON DIED FOR YOU. DON'T YOU KNOW HOW MUCH I CARE?"

CHAPTER 15

TOOTH FAIRIES, LEPRECHAUNS, AND ANGELS

When I was small, my mother told me about the tooth fairy. If a tooth came out, I was in luck. I put the tooth under my pillow and "Bingo!" I hit the jackpot. There under my pillow was a quarter! In those days, with a quarter, people could buy a Coke and a candy bar and have change. I'm not sure how it happened, but somehow, I learned there was no such thing as a tooth fairy.

I also remember believing in other imaginary characters like leprechauns. Every Irishman is familiar with that fellow. He is a tricky old man with a twinkle in his eye, but I soon learned he was also just a fictitious fairy.

Then, I became a Christian. I heard that some believers believed in guardian angels and even demons. Now, I was willing to believe in God. I was even willing to believe in the miracles of the Bible, but I wasn't sure about believing in angels. At the time, I thought to myself, "Now that is where I draw the line." I have been fooled once or twice, but not this time.

Do you believe in tooth fairies, leprechauns, and angels? I must confess that I do not believe in tooth fairies or leprechauns, but I've come to believe in angels and demons.

God Created Angels

God Created Angels No one can prove that angels exist, but then no one can prove that they do not exist. If you believe the Bible is the Word of God and, therefore, true, you are forced to believe in the existence of angels.

The Bible teaches that God created the heavens and the earth, providing a detailed account in one chapter (Gen. 1). Similarly, it describes God's creation of humans in another chapter (Gen. 2), but angels are only mentioned briefly. Nowhere are we told about their creation. We do know, however, that God created all things (Gen. 1:1; Jn. 1:3; Col. 1:16). So, since angels appear on the pages of Scripture, we must conclude that God created them. By not recording the act of creating angels, the Bible is telling us that they are not of major importance, but they are important enough for God to let us know they are there.

When a man talks about his family, he tells how he and his wife met and about the birth of his children. In the conversation, he might also mention that he has a dog. By not telling you about the dog's birth or how he got the dog, he might be subtly saying something, namely, that the dog is not as important as his children, but by at least mentioning the dog, he is saying that the dog is important and to know about his family you need to know about their dog. Likewise, angels are not the most important subject in the Bible, but they are there and we need to know about them.

Lewis Sperry Chafer says there are 273 references to angels in the Bible. Dr. Ryrie points out that angels are mentioned in at least 34 books of the Bible from the earliest to the last (Ryrie, *A Survey of Bible Doctrine*, p. 89).

Angels are Beings "What are these creatures like?" From the Scriptures, it can be stated with confidence that they are personal beings. A person is a being with intellect, emotions, and will. Angels have intelligence (1 Pet. 1:12), feelings (Lk. 2:13), and a will (Jude 6).

What are they like? Do they have wings, as shown in all the pictures depicting them? The answer is that they are spirit beings (Heb. 1:14), which leads to the conclusion that they do not have a body, at least a body of flesh and blood. Apparently, they do not have the power of reproduction. There is no such thing as a baby angel (Mk. 12:25), nor do they die (Lk. 20:36). Yet, they are always designated by the masculine gender (see Zech. 5:9 as a possible exception). They appear and people see them (Lk. 1:11-12). The Bible even says they have wings (Isa. 6:2). Angels are not the spirits of the departed, nor are they glorified human beings (Heb. 12:22-23).

Angels can be divided into two groups: the elect angels (1 Tim. 5:21), that is, those who did not follow Satan after he fell, and the evil angels who did follow Satan (Mt. 25:41).

Elect Angels

They are Ministers The elect angels are called ministering spirits (Heb. 1:14). To whom do they minister?

They minister to God. For example, the Seraphim worship Him (Isa. 6:1-3), and the cherubim guard His holiness (Gen. 3:22-24). There was an extra measure of angelic activity during our Lord's lifetime. They predicted His birth (Lk. 1:26-33), announced His birth (Lk. 2:13), protected Him as a baby (Mt. 2:13), strengthened Him after His temptation and again in the Garden of Gethsemane (Mt. 4:11; Lk. 22:43), and they rolled away the stone from the tomb and announced His resurrection (Mt. 28:2, 6).

They minister to nations. Angels minister not only to God but also to nations. Michael is Israel's guardian (Dan. 12:1). Apparently, other nations have angels assigned to them (Dan. 10:21). In this regard, angels also minister to unbelievers in carrying out God's will. An angel smote Herod (Acts 12:33). Angels will be involved in the judgments of the Tribulation Period (Rev. 8, 9, 16), and in separating the righteous from the wicked at the end of the Tribulation (Mt. 13:39).

They minister to believers. Two verses are used to teach that believers have guardian angels (Heb. 1:14; Mt. 18:10), but those verses do not necessarily teach believers to have their own guardian angels. They are just illustrations of angels ministering to believers. Angels are involved in answering prayer (Acts 12:7), encouraging in a time of danger (Acts 27:23-24), and caring for believers at death (Lk 16:22; Jude 9).

John Calvin said, "The angels are the dispensers and administrators of the divine beneficence towards us; they regard our safety, undertake our defense, direct our ways, and exercise a constant solicitude that no evil befall us."

The fact that angels minister to children (Mt. 18:10) explains how every little boy manages to reach adulthood. When a child gets to the climbing stage, it's then that every adult knows that an angel is on duty.

Just because angels minister to believers does not mean they protect them from all danger. As someone has pointed out, at 50 m.p.h., an angel rides on your hood. At 60 m.p.h., he closes his eyes. At 70 m.p.h., he gets off. At 80 m.p.h., he hums, "Nearer My God to Thee!"

They are Organized To accomplish that task, they are organized. Michael is the only angel designated as an archangel (Jude 9), though there must be others, for Daniel 10:13 says Michael is one of the chief princes. Under these chief angels, there are other angels (Eph. 3:10; 1 Pet. 3:22; Col. 1:16). Though the Bible does not give us enough information for us to have a detailed picture of the organization of angels, it does tell us there are cherubim, Seraphim, and living creatures. It also speaks of thrones, dominions, principalities, authorities, and powers.

If angels need to be organized to do God's will, so do God's people. Christians sometimes put down organizations as if they were all bad. They say, "If you want what people can do, organize. If you want what Madison Avenue can do, advertise. If you want what God can do, agonize." There is no such antithesis in Scripture. God organized the host of heaven, Moses organized the itinerants of Israel and Paul organized Christians into churches. If you want to carry out God's will in your family or in your life, you need to be organized.

Evil Angels

A second major group of angels is called fallen angels or evil angels. This group can be subdivided into Satan, demons, and imprisoned angels.

Satan What was the origin of Satan? Some expositors teach that Isaiah 14 and Ezekiel 28 describe Satan's origin and fall. According to that interpretation, Satan was a created angel (Ezek. 28:13, 14; Mt. 12:24). He was a cherub (Ezek. 28:14). He had a privileged position (Ezek. 28:14) and was called perfect (Ezek. 28:14). Then, he sinned (Ezek. 28:15). Isaiah 14 describes his fall as "I will ... I will ... I will ... I will ... I will." Paul calls it pride by its rightful name (1 Tim. 3:6).

I once taught that view because that was the interpretation I was taught in seminary. I had not personally studied Isaiah or Ezekiel. After examining those books, I concluded that Isaiah 14 and Ezekiel 28 do not refer to Satan. If that is the case, no passage reveals the origin of Satan. Calvin said, "Some persons grumble that Scripture does not, in numerous passages, set forth systematically and clearly that fall of the devils, its cause, manner, time, and character. But because this has nothing to do with us, it was better not to say anything, or at least to touch upon it lightly, because it did not befit the Holy Spirit to feed our curiosity with empty histories to no effect."

Satan's purpose is to oppose God, His program, and His people. The name "Satan" means "adversary." He tried to prevent God's program of redemption by influencing Peter (Mt. 16:23) and even by entering into Judas (Jn. 13:27). He blinds the minds of unbelievers (2 Cor. 4:4), so that they cannot understand the gospel. When the seed of the Word is planted in the heart of a person, Satan, like a bird plucking food from the earth, snatches it away (Lk. 8:12). He slanders (the word "devil" means "slanderer") believers, tempts them to lie (Acts 5:3), and commit immorality (1 Cor. 7:5).

Satan is the father of lies. Jesus said, "You are of your father the devil, and the desires of your father you want to do. He was a murderer from the beginning, and does not stand in the truth, because there is no truth in him. When he speaks a lie, he speaks from his own resources, for he is a liar and the father of it" (Jn. 8:44).

There is no indication in the Bible that Satan has horns, a tail, hoofs, a pitchfork, or a red suit.

When Satan fell, some of the angels followed him instead of God (Mt. 25:41). Satan is the prince of demons (Mt. 12:24). In fact, the definition of the doctrine of Satan is: Satan is an angel who fell and led other angels away from the service of God. These fallen angels are called demons. Demons can be divided into two categories: imprisoned demons and active demons.

Imprisoned Demons There is no question that the Bible teaches that some angels are in prison (2 Pet. 2:4; Jude 6), but there is a great debate concerning when and how it happened. Some maintain that the sons of God in Genesis 6 are angels who lusted after the daughters of men and thus left their own abode to come down and cohabit with them. As punishment, the theory says, God imprisoned them.

Others disagree with that theory. They say the sons of God in Genesis 6 are the godly line of Seth. They would say that 2 Peter and Jude are referring to angels who followed Satan in his original rebellion against God. If this view is correct, why were some imprisoned and others not? However they got there, Scripture teaches that some of the fallen angels are imprisoned.

Active Demons The second group of demons is not imprisoned. They are loose and active. The very fact that they are called Satan's angels (Mt. 24:41) indicates they do his bidding. Satan opposes God, so these demons aid Satan in his opposition of God's program and purpose.

These demons also influence nations. Daniel 10:13 speaks of "the prince of the kingdom of Persia." This passage seems to teach that a spiritual being (a demon) resisted an angel who brought Daniel a message. Revelation 16:13-14 indicates evil spirits will deceive nations in the Tribulation Period. Ryrie concludes, "A fair conclusion from these passages is simply that there is cosmic warfare involving the nations of the earth, and some demons are powerful enough to sway the affairs of nations. What this may mean in international affairs is not easy to discern. But that it means something significant, even today, seems clear" (Ryrie, *A Survey of Bible Doctrine*, p. 98).

Demons affect unbelievers. They inflict disease (Mt. 9:33; Lk. 13:11, 16), possess people (Mt. 8:28), and promote false doctrine (2 Tim. 4:1). They also attack God's people (Eph. 6:12).

In Ephesians 6, Paul tells believers that they wrestle against wicked spiritual forces (Eph. 6:12) and, therefore, should put on the whole armor of God (Eph. 6:13). He names the armor truth, righteousness, the gospel of peace, faith, the Word, and prayer (Eph. 6:14-18). Notice that the first piece of armor is truth. Remember, Satan is the father of lies.

In Ephesians 4, Paul warns, "Therefore, putting away lying, let each one of you speak truth with his neighbor, for we are members of one another. Be angry, and do not sin: do not let the sun go down on your wrath, nor give place to the devil" (Eph. 4:25-27). If you sin, including lying and letting the sun go down on your anger, you have given Satan and his demons a beachhead to stink up your life.

A Haitian pastor told a parable. He said a man wanted to sell his house for $2,000. Another man was eager to buy it, but he couldn't afford the full price due to his poverty. After much bargaining, the owner agreed to sell the house for half the original price with just one stipulation: he would retain ownership of one small nail protruding from just over the door.

After several years, the original owner wanted the house back, but the new owner was unwilling to sell. So first, the owner went out, found the carcass of a dead dog, and hung it from the nail he still owned. Soon, the house became uninhabitable, and the family was forced to sell it to the owner of the nail.

The Haitian pastor's conclusion: "If we leave the Devil with even one small peg in our life, he will return to hang his rotting garbage on it, making it unfit for Christ's habitation" (Dale A. Hays, *Leadership*, vol. 4, no. 2).

Summary: The Bible teaches that there are beings called angels. Some are elect and do God's bidding, while others are evil and do Satan's bidding, which is to oppose God. The doctrine of angels is that angels are an order of beings, which God created, some of which serve Him and others of which serve Satan (Heb. 1:14; Mt. 24:41).

Although it doesn't say much, the Bible does offer us a few words here and there about our relationship with angels. God wants us to know they exist, but He does not want us to communicate with them. He certainly does not want believers to worship angels, even the good ones (Col. 2:18). As for demons, God certainly does not want believers communicating with them (Eph. 4:27). To be specific, a believer should beware of ouija boards, séances, etc. James 4:7 says to resist the devil and he will flee from you.

Carlos Santana won eight Grammy awards for his album *Supernatural*, which has sold more than 10 million copies. A *Rolling Stone* profile of Santana describes Santana's spirituality:

> His meditation spot is in front of the fireplace.... A card with the word Metatron is spelled out in intricately painted picture letters and lies on the floor next to the fireplace. Metatron is an angel. Santana has been in regular contact with him since 1994. Carlos will sit here facing the wall, the candles lit. He has a yellow legal pad at one side, ready for the communications that will come. "It's kind of like a fax machine," he says....
>
> There are few conversations with [Santana] that don't lead to a discussion of angels or of the spiritual radio through which music comes.

Santana has been increasingly engaged by angels since the day in 1988 when he picked up a book on the subject at the Milwaukee airport. "It's an enormous peace, the few times I have felt the presence in the room," he says....

"My reality is that God speaks to you every day. There's an inner voice, and when you hear it, you get a little tingle in your medulla oblongata at the back of your neck, a little shiver, and at two o'clock in the morning, everything's really quiet, you meditate, you got the candles, you got the incense, and you've been chanting, and all of a sudden you hear this voice: Write this down. It is just an inner voice, and you trust it. That voice will never take you to the desert."...

Santana credits Metatron with alerting him to the recent changes in his life ("The Epic Life of Carlos Santana," Chris Heath, April 16, 2000, p. 41).

God does say, "Be sure to entertain strangers for they might be angels" (Heb. 13:2; see Gen. 18:1-8 for an illustration), but even if believers were to entertain an angel, they are not seeking communication. In fact, the writer to the Hebrews speaks of doing it "unwittingly."

Paul says angels are watching us! "For I think that God has displayed us, the apostles, last, as men condemned to death; for we have been made a spectacle to the world, both to angels and to men" (1 Cor. 4:9; 1 Tim. 5:21).

A mother writes, "My first-grade daughter, Jenny, loves to sing. One day, as I drove her to school, we were 'accompanying' Michael W. Smith on his song, 'Angels Unaware.' When we got to the line, 'Maybe we are entertaining angels unaware,' I heard her version loud and clear: 'Maybe we are irritating angels unaware.' I couldn't have said it better myself" (Nancy LaDuke, "Kids of the Kingdom," *Christian Reader*).

CHAPTER 16

AN OUTLINE OF THINGS TO COME

There are three levels of knowledge of Bible doctrine. At level one, people can describe a particular doctrine. At level two, they can demonstrate it. At level three, they can defend it.

For example, what is needed for salvation? Believers with level one knowledge will say, "Believe on the Lord Jesus Christ," but they cannot go beyond that; they cannot show where the Bible says that.

Believers with level two knowledge would say that the answer to the question is, "Believe on Christ," and they could take you to the Bible and show you where it says that, for example, John 3:16.

Believers with level three knowledge would say that the answer to the salvation question is, "Believe on Christ." They would also know that truth is taught in John 3:16. If someone objected and said, "No, you must work your way to heaven," this person with third-level knowledge of this doctrine would be able to take them to Ephesians 2:8-9 and show that works are not necessary for salvation.

How much do you know about prophecy? Most Christians don't know much. Those in a Bible-teaching church, however, are aware that there will be a Rapture, a Tribulation, and even a Millennium of rule by Christ on the earth. That would be level one knowledge of the Bible doctrine of prophecy. Not many Christians can go to level two. Could you? Could you take a Bible and show another person where it says a Tribulation will follow a Rapture? Could you prove Christ comes after that? Could you demonstrate from the Scriptures that He will reign on the earth for 1,000 years? Several of the major events of things to come are outlined in one passage of Scripture. Let's begin the discussion of prophecy with that passage.

The Tribulation

Jesus In Matthew 24:4-14, Jesus describes the end of the age. He says it will be a period (see "beginning" in Mt 24:8 and "end" in Mt. 24:14) characterized by false Christs (Mt. 24:4-5), as well as war (Mt. 24:6-7). There will be the reality and the rumor of war. The period Jesus describes will also be marked by natural disasters (Mt. 24:7), including empty cupboards, epidemics, and earthquakes. Persecutions will also take place (Mt. 24:9-10). There will be tormentors from without and traitors from within. In the midst of the chosen ones, the successor of Judas will be found, who will betray the disciples as he betrayed the Lord. There will be a general spiritual decline (Mt. 24:11-13). Sadly, at any time, there would be false prophets; during this period, it would be doubly sad, for there would be many. Their chilling and killing doctrine will take its toll. As deception increases, devotion will decrease. This period that Jesus describes in Matthew 24 is called the Tribulation Period (Mt. 24:29).

Other Passages Other passages give us more details. Daniel indicates it will last seven years (Dan. 9:25-27). John confirms that (Rev. 11:2, 3; 12:6, 14; 13:5). The Tribulation will witness the rise of the anti-Christ, called the "Little Horn" in Daniel 7 and the "King of Fierce Countenance" in Daniel 8. He is also called the beast by John in Revelation 13 and the man of sin by Paul (2 Thess. 2:3).

The Tribulation Period will not only witness the rise of the anti-Christ, but it will also see the fall of the wrath of God. Revelation 6 describes it as a time of war (Rev. 6:4), famine (Rev. 6:5-6), and persecution (Rev. 6:9), and concludes that it is a time of the wrath of God (Rev. 6:16-17).

The definition of the Tribulation is a period of judgment lasting seven years and covering the whole earth before the Second Coming of Jesus Christ (Mt. 24:4-14, 29-30).

After The Tribulation, Christ Will Return

Jesus After the Tribulation, the Lord will return to the earth. Jesus says, "Immediately after the tribulation of those days, the sun will be darkened, and the moon will not give its light; the stars will fall from heaven, and the powers of the heavens will be shaken. Then the sign of the Son of Man will appear in heaven, and then all the tribes of the earth will mourn, and they will see the Son of Man coming on the clouds of heaven with power and great glory" (Mt. 24:29-30). Notice, "Immediately after the tribulation," the Son of Man will come.

The Second Coming of Christ will be the most spectacular, sensational, and stupendous event in all of the history of the universe. Anything TV, Hollywood, or Disney World has ever done will be like striking a match as compared to a bolt of lightning. There will be darkness, dramatic, and total darkness (Mt. 24:29). The darkness will be followed by a bright, brilliant light (Mt. 24:30).

Remember a thunderstorm in the midst of a summer night? There were thick, dark clouds. The wind was blowing and howling. There was an eerie feeling in the air. Then, all of a sudden, there was a clap of thunder and a bolt of lightning. The sky, for a split second, lit up like noonday. That is a small glimpse of what it will be like. In total darkness, there will be the bright shining glory of the coming of Christ.

The problem is that all of this sounds sudden, but evidently, it will be gradual. Matthew 24:30 says, "All the tribes of the earth will see Him." That has led some to the conclusion that His coming will extend over many hours. If He descends gradually, then as the earth rotates, the entire world will be able to see Him as He approaches.

Other Passages Much, much more could be said about the Second Coming of Christ. For example, He will arrive on the Mount of Olives (Zech. 14:3-4), and it will split in two. All the tribes of the earth will mourn because Christ is coming in judgment.

The great contrast, however, is between the first coming and the Second Coming. The first time, He came as a lamb to die and to save. The second time, He will come as a lion to judge and rule. The definition of the second coming is that Jesus Christ will literally and physically return to the earth after the Tribulation and before His 1,000-year reign on the earth (Mt. 24:29-30).

After Christ Returns, He Will Reign

Jesus Matthew 24:30 says the Son of Man will come "with power and great glory." What follows is a series of applications. By parable and by preaching, the Lord says, in essence, "Get ready." Then, in Matthew 25:31, He picks up again with the Son of Man coming in glory. So, Matthew 25:31 picks up where Matthew 24:30 leaves off.

Now, Matthew 25:31 says, "Then He will sit on the throne of His glory." The point is that after He returns, He reigns, that is, He rules on the earth. Theologically, this is called the Millennium, which is simply a Latin word that means 1,000 years. How do we know He will rule for 1,000 years? This verse says He will sit on the throne. The answer to that is in another passage of Scripture.

Other Passages The book of Revelation describes the Second Coming of Jesus Christ in chapter 19. Then, Revelation 20:1-3 says the Lord will rule on the earth for 1,000 years. Some have objected to this teaching, pointing out that Revelation is a highly symbolic book and that Revelation 20 is a highly symbolic passage. After all, it is a vision consisting of a bottomless pit, a chain, and a dragon. How do we know that the 1,000 years is not symbolic, too?

There are no doubt symbols in the passage, but there is also interpretation within the vision. Revelation 20:2 says, "The dragon, that serpent of old who is the devil and Satan, and bound him for 1,000 years." The dragon is the vision part of the passage; the devil is the interpretation. Now, notice carefully that the 1,000 years is in the interpretation part (Rev. 20:2). Furthermore, this is a vision and no one can see 1,000 years. So, the 1,000 years must be interpretation. Thus, the Lord will reign on the earth for 1,000 years.

Other passages give us other details. This will be a time of universal spiritual perception. The knowledge of the Lord will fill the earth, as will peace and prosperity.

Shortly after I became a Christian, I heard of this doctrine for the first time. I thought to myself, "If my friends find out that I believe this, they will think I am nuts." The truth is that some of the finest minds in the history of the world have dreamed of such a day as the Millennial reign of Christ, including Plato's *Republic*, Moore's *Utopia*, and Bacon's *New Atlantis*. Even Lyndon Baines Johnson said in a speech that his "Great Society" called for "the abolishment of poverty, the conquering of disease, the total abolition of war and the lengthening of man's life to 150 or even 200 years." Listen, Lyndon, when Jesus comes, all that will be true and more.

The Millennium is defined as a 1,000-year rule of Jesus Christ on the earth (Mt. 25:31; Rev. 20:1-3).

Let's put all of this together. The Olivet Discourse in Matthew 24 and 25 outlines three major events of the coming prophecy. Matthew 24:29 tells of the Tribulation. Matthew 24:30 clearly says that Christ will come immediately after the Tribulation. Matthew 25:31 teaches He will sit on His throne after that, which means He will rule on the earth for 1,000 years.

The Rapture is Before the Tribulation

What about the Rapture? Doesn't the Bible teach that Christians will be removed from the earth? The answer, of course, is "Yes" (1 Thess. 4:15-18). The question is when. There are three possible answers: 1) before the Tribulation, 2) in the middle of the Tribulation, 3) after the Tribulation. Which answer is correct? (After this was originally written, the Pre-Wrath view was proposed.)

In the Greek text, verse 36 begins with "now concerning" (peri de), a construction that introduces a new subject (22:31; Mk. 12:26; 13:32; Acts 21:25; 1 Cor 7:1; 8:1; 12:1; 16:1,12;

1 Thess. 4:9, 13; 5:1). It is obvious that the Lord is abruptly saying something different. Until now, He has been saying that we can know (24:33), but now He says no one knows!

Later in Matthew 24, Jesus says, "But as the days of Noah *were*, so also will the coming of the Son of Man be. For as in the days before the flood, they were eating and drinking, marrying and giving in marriage, until the day that Noah entered the ark, and did not know until the flood came and took them all away, so also will the coming of the Son of Man be. Then two *men* will be in the field: one will be taken and the other left. Two *women will be* grinding at the mill: one will be taken and the other left. Watch, therefore, for you do not know what hour your Lord is coming" (Mt. 24:36-42).

In the Greek text, verse 36 begins with "now concerning" (*peri de*), a construction that introduces a new subject (22:31; Mk. 12:26; 13:32; Acts 21:25; 1 Cor 7:1; 8:1; 12:1; 16:1,12; 1 Thess. 4:9, 13; 5:1). It is obvious that the Lord is abruptly saying something different. Until now, He has been saying that we can know (24:33), but now He says no one knows!

Matthew 14:36-42 refers to the Rapture, not the end of the Tribulation. For one thing, the context indicates that this is not a reference to the end of the Tribulation. The end of the Tribulation is so bad that unless those days be shortened, no one would be saved (Mt. 24:22). Yet Matthew 24:38 indicates that what is being talked about here is the activities of ordinary life. Furthermore, there are signs preceding the Second Coming. Here, the whole point is that there are no signs.

Another indication that this is a reference to the rapture is that the Greek word translated "coming" (*parousia*) in Matthew 24:3, 27, 37, 39 means "presence, coming, arrival" (see comments on

24:3). It is roughly similar to the English word "advent." As the first advent was not just an arrival, but an arrival and a subsequent presence, the second advent is not just an arrival, but an arrival and a subsequent presence. The Second Advent begins at the time when God's judgment begins. As Matthew 24:37 says, the coming (*parousia*) of the Son of Man will be like the coming of the flood in Noah's day (Hodges, p. 25). The expression "in the days of the Son of Man" in Luke 17:26, which is a descriptive of a period of time, not a momentary event, is the same idea as "the coming (*parousia*) of the Son of Man" in Matthew 24:37. In other words, Jesus is going back to before the Tribulation and is talking about the Rapture. For Jesus to go back to the beginning of the Tribulation would not be unusual; in Matthew 24:15, He went back to the middle of the Tribulation.

Another indication of the Rapture is that the Greek word translated "taken" (airo) in Matthew 24:39 is a reference to being swept away in judgment, but the one rendered "taken" (*paralambano*) in Matthew 24:40-41 is different. It means "to take to or with oneself" (A-S), "to take into close association, take (to oneself), take with/along" (BDAG see also 1:20-21; 2:13, 14, 20, 21; 17:1). It is used of the Rapture in John 14:3!

Also, consider that the illustration Jesus uses is what happened "before the flood" (24:28).

In other words, Jesus is going back to before the Tribulation and is talking about the Rapture. For Jesus to go back to the beginning of the Tribulation would not be unusual; in Matthew 24:15, He went back to the middle of the Tribulation.

Imminency The New Testament teaches the doctrine of imminency. There is a difference between something being "soon" and something being "imminent." "Soon" means "before long, shortly, quickly, promptly, as soon as possible." "Imminent" means "impending, likely to happen." The New Testament does not necessarily teach that Jesus Christ will come soon. It does teach that the Rapture is imminent. It is pending, but it might not necessarily be immediate.

Passage after passage pictures the Lord's coming as imminent. James 5:8 says, "For the coming of the Lord is at hand." That is a clear statement of the doctrine of imminency. Even a commentator like Mitton, who did not believe in the Pre-tribulation Rapture, said about this verse, "James believed, as others of his time did, that the coming of Christ was imminent."

Paul expected the Rapture to take place in his lifetime. First Thessalonians 4:15 says, "For this, we say to you by the word of the Lord that *we* who are alive and remain until the coming of the Lord will by no means precede those who are asleep."

Dean Alford, the famous Greek commentator of the nineteenth century, said on this passage, "Then beyond question, he himself expected to be alive, together with a majority of those to whom he was writing, at the Lord's coming."

Frame, another famous commentator on 1 Thessalonians, said, "Paul thus betrays the expectation that he and his contemporary Christians will remain alive until Christ comes."

Milligan, who wrote a classic commentary on 1 Thessalonians, says, "There can be no doubt that the passage naturally suggests that they expected so to survive ... and we must not allow the fact that they were mistaken in this belief to deprive their words of their proper meaning.... How far, indeed, an interpreter may go in the supposed interest of the apostolic infallibility is shown by the attitude amongst [sic] others of Calvin who thinks that the apostles used the first person simply in order to keep the Thessalonians on the alert."

One must either conclude that the writers of the New Testament were mistaken or that they expected the imminent return of Christ. There are signs for His Second Coming after the Tribulation, but there are no signs in the passages that talk about the Rapture. In other words, the first-century believers were not looking for signs but for the Son. They were not looking for the Tribulation but listening for the trumpet.

The Wrath of God A second reason for believing that the Lord will rapture the church before the Tribulation has to do with what the New Testament says about the wrath of God. First Thessalonians 1:10 says, "And to wait for His Son from heaven, whom He raised from the dead, even Jesus, who delivers us from the wrath to come." According to this passage, Christ will come and deliver us from the wrath to come. Later in 1 Thessalonians, Paul says, "God did not appoint us to wrath" (1 Thess. 5:9). The Bible is clear that the church will not experience the wrath of God. Almost all, regardless of their position on prophecy, agree with that. What some tend to overlook is that the Tribulation Period is the time of God's wrath (Rev. 6:15-17; 11:16-18; 15:1; 16:19). If the church will not experience the wrath of God, and if the Tribulation is the time of God's wrath, the church will not go through the Tribulation.

Other Arguments Many other arguments have been advanced for the Pre-tribulation Rapture. For example, the Lord promised the church at Philadelphia that He would keep them "from the hour of trial which shall come upon the whole world to test those who dwell on the earth" (Rev. 3:10).

A definition of the Rapture is the supernatural taking away of all church saints before the Tribulation (1 Thess. 4:13-18; Rev. 3:10).

Summary: An outline of things to come is: 1) The Lord will rapture the church (Mt. 24:36-42), 2) There will be a period of Tribulation (Mt. 24:29), 3) The Lord will return after the Tribulation (Mt. 24:30), 4) The Lord will reign on the earth (Mt. 25:31).

Those four statements and references should give any believer a level two knowledge of the doctrine of biblical prophecy.

Jesus says, "Know this, that if the master of the house had known what hour the thief would come, he would have watched and not allowed his house to be broken into. Therefore, you also be ready, for the Son of Man is coming at an hour you do not expect. 'Who then is a faithful and wise servant, whom his master made ruler over his household, to give them food in due season? Blessed *is* that servant whom his master, when he comes, will find so doing. Assuredly, I say to you that he will make him ruler over all his goods. But if that evil servant says in his heart, 'My master is delaying his coming,' and begins to beat *his* fellow servants, and to eat and drink with the drunkards, the master of that servant will come on a day when he is not looking for *him* and at an hour that he is not aware of, and will cut him in two and appoint *him* his portion with the hypocrites. There shall be weeping and gnashing of teeth (Mt. 24:43-51).

CHAPTER 16

WHAT HAPPENS AFTER DEATH?

Perhaps one of the first questions humans asked was, "What happens after death?" Everybody, regardless of age, has asked it for as long as people have been on the earth. It is still being asked today, every day, everywhere. It is one of the most basic questions in life.

That question was asked early. One of the first men to live on the earth was Job. He asked, "If a man dies, shall he live again?" (Job 14:14). That question has been asked often. Anthropologists and historians have found that every culture and civilization has had opinions and views about what happens after death. That question is asked today. You have probably asked it. What is the answer to the question, "What happens after death?" There are several possible answers to the question.

Annihilation

The Position Some say that when people die, there is nothing; they are annihilated. An Agnostic says, "I think." They lack certain knowledge and don't believe in the existence of anything after death. Atheists say, "It seems to me." They claim there is no evidence. So, they do not believe in God or life after death. Antagonists say, "In my opinion." In their opinion, there is no proof of life after death and, thus, no hope.

Atheist Madelyn Murray O'Hair is reported to have said: "The business of the public schools, where attendance is compulsory, is to prepare children to face the problems on earth, not to prepare for heaven, which is a delusional dream of the unsophisticated minds of the ill-educated clergy."

To her and many others, when we die, that's it. After death, there is nothing. Death is a dead end.

The Rebuttal Yet, David said, "I will dwell in the house of the Lord forever" (Ps. 23:6). Jesus announced, "In My Father's house are many mansions. If it were not so, I would have told you. I go to prepare a place for you, and if I go and prepare a place for you, I will come again and receive you to Myself, that where I am there, you may be also" (Jn. 14:2-3). Now, you can take the speculations of mere mortals or the authoritative statement of the Son of God.

Those who say that it's all over after death are like the man who attended the Metropolitan Opera. Thinking the intermission was the end of the program, he rose from his seat, picked up his hat and coat, and commented on the quality of the opera. A few minutes later, he learned, to his extreme embarrassment, that the performance was only half over.

Many are like that man in thinking that when the body is handed to the mortician, the play is over. According to Scripture, that is not the case. It is only an intermission; the play has only begun.

Reincarnation

The Position The second theory of what happens at death is called reincarnation. This view says that the soul passes into another body here on earth. The new body may be either animal or human.

This view is ancient. The ancient Egyptians are said to have practiced embalming to prevent or delay reincarnation. Even Plato believed in reincarnation. According to him, the soul is immortal, but the number of souls is fixed and reincarnation regularly occurs. One wonders how he would explain the significant population growth since his time. Aristotle, by the way, rejected Plato's teachings.

While reincarnation has its roots in ancient cultures and is found among some primitive tribes even today, it is most popular in India. According to Hinduism, as soon as people die, they are reborn and are either punished for all the evil they have done or rewarded for all the good. That concept is peculiar to Hinduism. Hinduism says, "The end of birth is death, and the end of death is birth." The body is like a garment. When it becomes outworn through age or idleness, the soul leaves it and is reincarnated in the body of a newborn baby.

According to Buddhism, a transition period of 49 days between death and rebirth is postulated. During this state, the individual is translated to a realm where he perceives divine secrets. These are so frightening that the individual falls back to earth and is reborn in another physical life.

I once met a man in Canada who had been heavily influenced by Eastern thought. He strongly believed that all life was sacred and that reincarnation was a fact. Therefore, he objected even to the killing of a fly because, in his opinion, among other things, that fly in a previous life was a person.

The Rebuttal The answer to reincarnation is revelation. Ecclesiastes 12:7 says, "Then the dust will return to the earth, as it was, and the spirit will return to God." The man who wrote those words was said to be the wisest man on earth (1 Kings 4:29-31).

Besides, he wrote under the inspiration of the Spirit of God (2 Tim. 3:16). God also says, "And as it is appointed for men to die once, but after this, the judgment" (Heb. 9:27). Notice there is one death and *then* the judgment, not reincarnation. There will be no opportunity to rectify the mess people have made during their lifetime.

Death is a river across which there is only one-way traffic. When Hamlet wonders whether life is worth living and has various reasons for thinking it isn't, he concludes he had better go on where he was rather than try out "the undiscovered country from whose barrier no traveler returns."

Soul Sleep

The Position The third view is called soul sleep. The doctrine of soul sleep teaches that the soul sleeps between death and the resurrection. This theory uses Scripture to prove its position. The proponents of soul sleep point to the use of "sleep" to refer to death and contend that death is sleep. They also use such passages as Ecclesiastes 9:5, 10 and Psalm 6:5.

The Rebuttal Granted, the Bible uses the word sleep to refer to death, but that is a figure of speech not to be taken literally. Furthermore, it is the body that sleeps and not the soul. That is evident from the fact that Abraham and Lazarus, as well as the rich man across the great gulf, were not asleep after their death and burial (Lk. 16:25), nor were Moses and Elijah asleep when they met Jesus on the Mount of Transfiguration (Mt. 17:3). When the book of Revelation pulls back the curtain and allows its readers a glimpse of heaven, it pictures the saints speaking and singing (Rev. 6:9-11, etc.). Clearly, "sleep" is the death condition of the body and not of the soul.

When a passage like Ecclesiastes 9:5 says "that the dead know nothing," it means that the dead take no part in the affairs of earth. Solomon never intended for a person to understand by his statement in chapter 9 that the soul sleeps after death because later in his book, he says that at death, the spirit returns to God (Eccl. 12:7). When David said in Psalm 6:5, "for in death there is no remembrance of You; in the grave, who will give You thanks?" he did not intend to teach soul sleep. As Alexander says in his commentary on this verse, "This verse does not prove that David had no belief or expectation of a future state, nor that the intermediate state is an unconscious one, but only that in this emergency, he looks no further than the close of life, as the appointed term of thanksgiving and praise. Whatever might eventually follow, his death would certainly put an end to the praise of God in that form in those circumstances to which he had been accustomed."

Purgatory

The Position The Roman Catholic Church says that after death, a Catholic goes to purgatory. Purgatory is "The state, place or condition in the next world, which will continue until the last judgment where the souls of those who die in the state of grace, but not yet free from all imperfection, make expiation for unforgiven venial sins or for the temporal punishment due to venial and mortal sins that have already been forgiven and, by so doing, are purified before they enter heaven" (*The New Encyclopedia*, 1967 edition, p. 1034).

The Rebuttal The Scripture knows of no such place. Moreover,

Jesus Christ told the thief on the cross, "Assuredly I say to you, today you will be with Me in paradise" (Lk. 23:43). Those words from the lips of the dying Savior put the deathblow to the doctrine of purgatory. If ever a sinner needed purging and cleansing in purgatorial flames in addition to the cleansing power of Jesus' blood, it was the dying thief. Yet, Jesus did not say, "Today, you will be in purgatory." He didn't even say, "Today, you will be in paradise." He said, "You will be *with Me* in paradise." Thus, after death, the believer does not go to purgatory, but paradise, yea, not paradise, but is ushered into the very presence of God.

By the way, the *Catholic Encyclopedia* admits that the Bible does not teach the doctrine of purgatory. It says, "According to the teaching of the church." Later, the same article says, "In the final analysis, the Catholic doctrine on purgatory is based on tradition, not sacred Scripture."

Immortality

The Position The Bible teaches immortality, that is, unending existence after death. It teaches the immortality of believers and unbelievers. When people die, they do not cease to exist permanently or temporarily. Nor do they come back to this life. They continue to live, though not in their earthly bodies or here, yet they do continue to live. Souls depart the body (Gen. 35:18) and go somewhere else.

A suicidal fellow once called Sam Shoemaker and said, "I'm going to end my life." Sam responded, "You can't do that!" The fellow replied, "Sure, I can!" Sam said, "No, you can't." When the fellow insisted he could, Sam said, "You can get a transfer, but you can't end your life." That's the doctrine of immortality.

Every human lives forever, but not all go to the same place. The Bible teaches that believers, upon death, go immediately to be with the Lord (Phil. 1:23; 2 Cor. 5:8; Lk. 23:43; Acts 7:56; etc.). Unbelievers go to hell (Lk. 16:19-31).

To eliminate the doctrine of hell, some have charged that the account of the rich man and Lazarus in Luke 16 is a parable, but such is not the case. Parables are made-up stories with characters who do not have names, and this story contains individuals with names. Even if the incident in Luke 16 was a parable, the Lord still teaches the doctrine of hell. If annihilation or soul sleep is true, Jesus taught false doctrine by telling this story.

Summary: According to the Bible, immediately upon death, every human being goes somewhere else forever. Saints, those who have trusted Jesus Christ as their Savior, live forever and so do sinners; the only difference is the place of their eternal abode.

Therefore, the definition of the doctrine of immortality is: all humans have unending existence after death (believers go to be with the Lord—Phil. 1:23; 2 Cor. 5:8; unbelievers go to hell—Lk. 16:19-21, then the Lake of Fire—Rev. 20:11-15). It is not the duration of life but the destination of life that counts. So prepare.

Two years before his death, Mike Hanzas, who lived alone, began to make preparations for his demise. He bought a plot in the cemetery. Weekly, he visited the site where his mortal remains would be interred. He planted grass and mowed it regularly. On Memorial Day, he planted flowers on the gravesite. He said, "I want to see the flowers there now. I will not be able to see them when I'm gone!"

Mike went into a funeral home. "I want to buy the casket that will be my new home," he said. Whenever he passed the funeral home, he would go in. Standing beside the casket, he would say, "That's where I'm going to live someday!"

One day, Mike invited a nephew and the rest of his family to visit him. After a hearty meal, Mike began to dispense canned goods and personal effects to his visitors. Then, he handed his nephew his will. As he did this, he dropped dead of heart failure!

So far as we know, Mike Hanzas had made every provision for his body but none for his soul. During this meticulous preparation, he failed to reckon with the fact that God would sometimes say to him, "This night thy soul shall be required of thee!"

CHAPTER 17

WHAT WILL HEAVEN BE LIKE?

What's heaven like? Will saints be dressed in white robes with a green leaf crown on their heads? What will they do with all that time? Lounge on a Posturepedic cloud, softly strumming "Sweet Isle of Somewhere" on a harp. Will it be like church, where saints sing long songs and listen to long sermons? Imagine that—forever!

Why do we have such a vague view and vision of heaven? Perhaps it is because more seems to be said about hell in the Bible than heaven.

Perhaps it is because preachers focus more on the Lake of Fire than the land of eternal bliss. At any rate, the fact is that the Bible does describe some things about heaven and you need to know what it says. Many people want to go to heaven simply because they are not thrilled with the alternative, but they don't know what they will be doing when they get there. You need to study what the Bible says about heaven to see what you've gotten yourself into by choosing that as your eternal destination.

Technically, the word heaven is used in three ways in the Bible: 1) The atmosphere (Mt. 24:30). The first heaven is where the birds and planes fly, clouds are formed and float along, and the smog lives. 2) The outer stratosphere (Mt. 24:29). The second heaven is where the sun, moon, planets, and stars are. It is commonly called outer space. 3) Paradise (Mt. 6:9; 24:36; 2 Cor. 12:2). The third heaven is the abode of God. The first heaven can be seen by day, the second by night, and the third by faith. It is the third heaven, which is the subject of this study.

Heaven is a Place

A Place Is heaven a real place? Some say, "No." In a six-hour PBS special, Bill Moyers interviewed Dr. Joseph Campbell (d. 1987 at 83), Professor, President of the American Society of the Study of Religion and author of *The Power of Myth*, the book that inspired *Star Wars*.

During the interview, Campbell said, "He who thinks he knows doesn't know. He who doesn't think he knows knows." He also said that the expression "our Father" in the Lord's Prayer is an analogy. We know that because the passage speaks of heaven, we know heaven is not a real place; it is an analogy. So, God being a Father is also an analogy.

In the Upper Room Discourse, the Lord twice told the disciples that He would prepare a *place* for them (Jn. 14:2-3). Luke records that after the resurrection, the Lord ascended and went to heaven (Acts 1:10-11). So, the Bible calls heaven, where Jesus went (Acts 1:10-11), a place (Jn. 14:2).

There you have it. It is either Jesus Christ or Joseph Campbell. Jesus said heaven is a place. Joseph Campbell said he knew it was not. Remember what he said about knowing? By his standard, he does not know.

Now, what kind of place is it? John 14:2 says there will be mansions there. The word translated "mansions" occurs only in the New Testament in John 14:2 and John 14:23, where it is translated "abode." The Greek word only means "abode." The rendering "mansions" comes from the Latin Vulgate. The Latin word meant "resting place," that is, a "station" on the road where travelers found refreshment. The famous Greek scholar Westcott says, "This appears to be the true meaning of the Greek word here."

The word "mansion" does not tell us much. It certainly does not mean what we think of today when we hear the word mansion. Some modern translations have chosen to translate the word with phrases like "dwelling places" or "rooms." While this Greek word in this Greek passage does not give us much information, other passages give us some insights.

A City The New Testament calls this place a city (Heb. 11:10; 2 Pet. 3:13; Rev. 21:1-4). It may surprise some saints to discover that the Bible teaches that believers will live in the New Jerusalem forever and that the New Jerusalem will rest on the new earth. Dr. Ryrie says, "This heavenly city will be the abode of all the saints ... the place He is preparing for His people.... It will be the dwelling place of all believers during eternity" (*Ryrie Study Bible* on Rev. 21:2). Dr. Louis Talbot once said, "This wonderful city is to be the everlasting home of all who have trusted the Lord Jesus Christ" (Talbot, *What the Bible Says About Heaven*, p. 17).

Heaven, then, is a real, literal place, a city. It is not a state of mind or a figment of the imagination. It is a city as real as New York, Chicago, or Los Angeles. It may be more real than those places, for those places are decaying.

Charles Fuller, a famous radio evangelist on the Old Fashioned Revival Hour, once announced on the radio that he would speak the next Sunday on heaven. The following week, he received a letter from Harry Rimmer, who was very ill. It read: "Next Sunday, you are to talk about 'Heaven.' I am interested in that land because I have held a clear title to a bit of property there for over 55 years. I did not buy it. It was given to me without money and without price. But the Donor purchased it for me at a tremendous sacrifice.

I am not holding it for speculation since the title is not transferable. It is not a vacant lot. For more than half a century, I have been sending material out of which the greatest architect and builder of the universe has been building a home for me, which will never need to be repaired because it will suit me perfectly individually and will never grow old. Termites can never undermine its foundation, for they rest upon the Rock of Ages. Fire cannot destroy it. Floods cannot wash it away. No locks or bolts will ever be placed upon its doors, for no vicious person can ever enter that land where my dwelling stands, now almost ready for me to enter in and abide in peace eternally, without fear of being ejected. There is a valley of deep shadows between the place where I live in California and that to which I shall journey in a very short time. I cannot reach my home in that city of God without passing through that dark valley of shadows. But I am not afraid, because the best Friend that I ever had went through the same valley long, long ago and drove away all its gloom. He has stuck by me through thick and thin and since we first became acquainted 55 years ago, I hold His promise in printed form, never to forsake nor to leave me alone. He will be with me as I walk through the valley of the shadows, and I shall not lose my way when He is with me. I hope to hear your sermon on 'Heaven' next Sunday from my home in Los Angeles, California, but I have no assurance that I shall be able to do so. My ticket to Heaven has no date marked for the journey—no return coupon—and no permit for baggage. Yes, I am all ready to go and I may not be here while you are talking next Sunday evening, but I shall meet you there someday" (compiled by J. D. Carlson).

Before this letter reached Charles Fuller, Harry Rimmer reached the place about which he wrote.

Heaven will be a Happy Place

No Sorrow Heaven will be a happy place, if for no other reason than because God is there, and the psalmist declares that in His presence is fullness of joy (Ps. 16:10). Beyond that, the Bible says explicitly that God will remove sorrow (Rev. 21:4, 5). Part of what will make heaven a fun place is that many of life's killjoys will not be there. God has promised believers a new body (1 Cor. 15:50) that will not need aspirin, band-aids, crutches, dentures, hearing aids, or heating pads. Life in heaven will be free of pain, tears, and death.

No Sin Heaven will also be a joyous place because God will remove sorrow and sinners (Rev. 21:8). The things that are killjoys on earth—selfishness, greed, hatred, death—will not be in heaven. The most joy-filled moments a person has in this life, minus any sadness, plus the presence of God, multiplied by infinity, is what heaven will be like.

Spectacular Beauty Heaven will be enjoyable because God will reveal spectacular beauty there (Rev. 21:9-21). A small boy looked up at the sky and said, "If this is what it looks like from the bottom, what must it look like from the top?"

A partial answer to the young lad's question is in Revelation 21. John describes the spectacular beauty of the New Jerusalem. This alone does not make heaven a happy place, but it will surely add pleasure. J. A. Seiss, who wrote one of the classic commentaries on the book of Revelation, states, "This city is a solid cube of golden construction, 1500 miles every way. Its base would stretch from the furthest Maine to the furthest Florida and from the shore of the Atlantic to Colorado. It would cover all of Britain, Ireland, France, Spain, Italy, Germany, Austria, Persia, European Turkey, and half of European Russia taken together! Stupendous magnitude!" (J. A. Seiss, *Apocalypse*, p. 498).

The late Dr. W. E. Biederwolf tells the story of a little girl, blind from birth, on whose eyes a noted surgeon performed a successful operation. As the scenes of the earth came into focus for the first time, she ran into her mother's arms and cried, "Oh, Mother, why didn't you tell me the world was so beautiful?" Her mother, wiping away her own tears, replied, "My child, I tried to tell you, but I couldn't do it. You had to see it for yourself."

When we see heaven for ourselves, we will no doubt turn to John and say, "Why didn't you tell us just how beautiful it was?" He will probably respond that he did the best he could, considering his human limitations. The truth is, we will have to see it for ourselves.

Heaven will not be dull. It will not be like a protracted chess game. It will be enjoyable and exciting, for God will remove the impurities and imperfections.

Heaven will be a Busy Place

Not Idle Perhaps the most common question concerning heaven is, "What will believers do there?" Some fear they will do nothing; thus, heaven will be a bore. Some young people fear it will be like a small town in the Midwest where they roll up the sidewalks at sundown and do nothing.

I once spoke in a tiny town in the state of Montana. The pastor of the church where I spoke had been a pastor in New York City. When my family and I arrived, it was late on a hot Saturday evening. The small town had a highway, two bars, and a couple of service stations. The two bars were open; the two stations were closed. One main street was perpendicular to the highway, with a few shops on either side. All those were also closed. The town was almost deserted. We called the pastor from a phone booth and he came to meet us. When he greeted us, he said, "Welcome to Montana." My teenage kids wanted to know what people did in such a small town. This transplanted big city pastor said, "Well, on Saturday night at sundown, we all gather at the filling station and watch the candy bars melt." Will heaven be that dull?

Industrious No! Saints will serve in heaven (Rev. 22:3). That fact alone assures us that we will be busy in heaven. The Bible does not choose to reveal to us the nature of our activities, but it does inform us that there will be something to do. As creative as God is, it is unthinkable that saints in heaven will do nothing.

Other passages peel back the curtain and give us a view of heaven. In those glimpses, there is always singing and worshiping. So saints will not just sit around heaven listening to their beards grow. Heaven is not a habitat for the idle or a haven for the lazy. There will be enjoyment and employment.

T. B. Talmage has said, "Many people suppose that we shall get to see and enjoy all of heaven the first day we arrive. However, you can't see London in two weeks, you cannot see Rome in six weeks, and you cannot see Venice in a month. Nor can you see the great city of God in a day! No, it will take all eternity to see heaven, count the towers, examine the trophies, gaze upon the thrones, and see the hierarchies. Ages on ages roll, and yet heaven is new. The streets are new! The joy is new! The song is new!"

Heaven will be a Populated Place

People The one other salient feature the Bible reveals about heaven is that it will be a populated place (Rev. 21:24). The Old Testament saints will be there: Adam and Abraham, Moses and Micah, Samson and Samuel, Isaiah and Isaac, Zephaniah and Zechariah. New Testament saints will include Peter and Paul, James and John, Mary and Martha. The saints of the ages will also be present: John Huss, John Wycliffe, John Calvin, and John Wesley; George Whitfield and George Muller; Charles Spurgeon and Charles Wesley; R. A. Torrey and Louis Talbot.

Your Christian friends and relatives will also be there. Heaven consists of a multitude of people—a multitude no person can number.

The Lord Best of all, the Lord will be there (Rev. 21:22-23; 22:3-4). The Lord Himself told the disciples that He would prepare a place for them, and if He did, He would come back and receive them unto Himself, that where He was, they might also be (Jn. 14:1-3). Paul said, "And so shall we ever be with the Lord" (1 Thess. 4:17). Heaven would not be heaven without the Lord.

A child who lost her mother became inconsolable. Her father sent her to another locality for a change of scenery. While she was gone, he built a beautiful house filled with rare and costly furniture. Then, he sent for his little girl and brought her into the house he had built, but he could not interest her in any part of it. When he would take her into a room, she would quickly look around and ask to be shown the next. At last, her father had to say, "My child, there are no more rooms. You have seen them all." Then she fell to the floor with a despairing cry, "Oh, Mama! Oh, Mama! This is not home without *you*!" As a house is not home without Mother, so heaven could never be our eternal home without the Lord Himself.

Ultimately, saints are not looking for golden streets. They're looking for His face. While it is true that heaven is a place, it is more than that. It is a person (Jn. 14:3; 1 Thess. 4:17), which is the ultimate excitement.

Summary: Heaven is a place, a happy, busy, populated place. There will be enjoyment, employment, and excitement there. The definition of the doctrine of heaven is that heaven is a place where all the children of God will spend eternity with their heavenly Father (Jn. 14:1-6; Rev. 21, 22).

The Lord reveals what little we know about heaven to challenge unbelievers to trust Christ (Jn. 14:1-6), to comfort the bereaved (1 Thess. 4:13-18), and to challenge believers (Mt. 6:20).

John Harper, a well-known English evangelist of his day, was a passenger on the ill-fated Titanic journeying to America to conduct an evangelistic campaign in the Moody Church of Chicago. The evening of the catastrophe, he was standing on the deck with a friend watching the sunset. The heavens were aglow with a picture that only God could paint. Harper turned to his friend and said, "It will be beautiful in the morning." A few hours later, the great ocean liner struck an iceberg, and Dr. Harper went from the sinking ship's deck into the Lord's presence. However, for him, "the morning" was indeed "beautiful." There's a glad and glorious morning ahead for every child of God.

CHAPTER 19

HELL? NO!

Being a preacher of the Bible is sometimes like being a physician. Both have to deliver both glad and sad news. When a healthy baby is born, the doctor announces good news. When a loved one passes away, the doctor has to report the sad news to the family. Likewise, a faithful teacher of the Bible has the privilege of announcing the happy news of heaven and must also warn of the reality of hell.

Is there a hell? If so, what is it like?

Many a "man on the street" would say, "Yes, there's a hell, all right. It's right here and now." His hell is his work or his wife. Shakespeare said, "To be with my conscience is hell enough for me."

Some theologians say, "Yes," but hell, according to them, is not here and now; it is somewhere else and later. It is not permanent but temporary. In this view, you are saved and safe after you suffer sufficiently. In other words, restoration follows a period of punishment.

Other theologians say, "Yes, there is a hell. Hell is somewhere else and later and eternal."

Universalist says, "No." According to them, God loves us, and He saves us all.

Annihilationists say, "No, we die like dogs and our souls perish with our bodies. There is no hell; there is no anything. After death, there is ultimate and final oblivion."

What do the Scriptures say?

Hell is a Place

A Prepared Place If the Bible could speak audibly, it would scream loudly, "There is a hell!" It is a definite and specific place (Lk. 10:15; 16:23). Matthew 25:41 says hell is a prepared place. The word translated "prepared" is the same one used for the kingdom (Mt. 25:34) and for the mansions of heaven (Jn. 14:2). Just as the Millennium on this earth and mansions in heaven are a place, so hell is a place. Hell is not a cuss word; it is a place. Hell is not a condition of the mind; it is a place.

An Eternal Place The next question is, "How long will it last?" "Will it last forever?" "Is hell eternal?" The answer to that question is "No" (Rev. 20:12-15; 21:8). Hell is the temporary abode of the wicked dead. The Lake of Fire is the permanent place of the wicked dead. Dr. Ryrie says, "Hades is temporary in that it will be cast into the Lake of Fire" (Ryrie, *Survey of Bible Doctrine*, p. 184).

Let me illustrate. A criminal is put into the local jail before he is put into the state penitentiary for life. Likewise, hell is the local jail; the Lake of Fire is the federal penitentiary. So, the question becomes, "Is the Lake of Fire eternal?" "Is there eternal separation from God?" The answer is "Yes" (Mt. 20:10; 25:46).

This doctrine has been challenged with the argument that the Greek word for "everlasting/eternal" does not necessarily imply endlessness, but the same Greek word used for eternal punishment (Mt. 25:46) is the same word used for eternal life (Mt. 25:46) and for the eternal God (1 Tim. 1:17). If one is temporary, the others must also be. Dr. Ryrie adds, "Furthermore, the same phrase that means 'forever' is used of God being alive forever (Rev. 15:7), of eternal life (Jn. 10:28), and of eternal torment (Rev. 14:11). There is no way to escape the conclusion that if God is everlasting, so is the punishment in the Lake of Fire" (Ryrie, *Survey of Bible Doctrine*, p. 184).

The Lake of Fire is a Place of Death

If the Lake of Fire is the place of eternal separation from God, what kind of place is it? What is the Lake of Fire like? For one thing, it is the place of death (Rev. 20:14). That does not mean annihilation (*cf.* Rev. 19:20 with 20:10). After the 1,000 years in the Lake of Fire, the beast and the false prophet are still there, personally existing.

What, then, does "death" mean? Death is separation. Physical death is the separation of the body and the soul. The second death is the separation of the soul from God. Thus, when the Bible says the Lake of Fire is the second death, it means it is eternal separation from God.

Revelation 21:1-8 also indicates that the Lake of Fire is separation from God (*cf.* esp. 21:3 with 21:7, and then 21:8). Heaven is where God is; hell is where God is not. First John 5:12 says that to have God is to have life. Not to have the Son is not to have life. In the presence of God, there is life: love, joy, peace, and praise. Away from God, there is no life, only existence: no life, no love, no peace, no praise.

The Lake of Fire is a Place of Darkness

The Lake of Fire is not only the place of death, that is, separation from God, it is also the place of darkness (Mt. 13:42, 50; 2 Pet.

2:17; Jude 13). First John 1:5 says that God is light. The Lake of Fire is primarily separation from God. Therefore, by the nature of the case, it is a separation from light.

The fact that hell will be separation from God doesn't bother some people. They think, "I'll be with my friends." They don't understand that hell is also a place of darkness. How will they find their friends and, if they could, how would they ever enjoy them in the dark?

Bob Jones, Sr., the famous southern evangelist, tells of a lady who trained her parakeet to say "Good night" and "Good morning." She would place the cover over the cage each evening and say, "Good night, Polly." The parakeet would reply, "Good night." She would lift the cover in the morning and say, "Good morning," and the parakeet would reply, "Good morning."

One day, the parakeet escaped from the cage and got into a fight with a cat. That night, the cage was covered, and the lady said, "Good night," as usual. However, when she lifted the cover the next morning, she said, "Good morning," and the parakeet replied, "Good night." Startled, the lady repeated the greeting and the parakeet again said, "Good night." She discovered that the bird had its eyes scratched out in the fight with the cat and he would never say "Good morning" again.

Hell is the eternal "good night" since the sun never rises in the land of anguish and despair (Robert Summer, *Hell Is No Joke*, p. 18).

The Lake of Fire is a Place of Distress

It may sound like saying the obvious, but the Lake of Fire is a place of fire (Rev. 20:10, 14; 21:8). Another Greek word for this Lake of Fire vividly indicates and illustrates that it contains fire. It is the Greek word *gehenna* (Mt. 18:9—*gehenna* is sometimes translated hell). *Gehenna* is the Valley of Hinnom. Jerusalem sits on several hills. On the south side of Jerusalem, there is a deep, narrow valley. In the first century, it was the refuse dump of Jerusalem, a kind of vast incinerator. Refuse was almost always burning there and a pillar of smoke and the smell of a smoldering fire surrounded it. It was the receptacle of all sorts of putrefying matter and mess. Such is the picture of hell.

So horrible is the picture of hell that many object, claiming the fire is figurative and not literal. My response is, "If you are going to hell, you should hope it is literal, because if it is figurative, it is worse than literal fire and the only way God could communicate it to human minds was to use fire as a figure."

Another common objection to the biblical doctrine of hell is, "How can anyone in a literal fire with a body not be destroyed?" Frankly, I don't know, but I do know it will happen (Rev. 19:20; 20:10). Remember, after the 1,000 years in the Lake of Fire, the beast and the false prophet still exist there undestroyed.

First John 4:8 says God is love. The opposite is hate. If heaven is the presence of God, who is love, then hell is a place of torment and hate. The inhabitants there will no doubt hate themselves more than anyone else.

The point is that the Lake of Fire is a place of fire and torment (Rev. 20:19; 16:24). The torment will be both physical and spiritual.

Summary: The Lake of Fire is an eternal place of separation from God, a place of darkness and conscious torment.

By definition, the doctrine of hell is that hell, and later, the Lake of Fire, is the place of torment for all those who do not trust Jesus Christ in this life (Rev. 20:14).

To many, that doctrine seems unfair, unjust, and unnecessary. Why so much torment and why so long?

In defense of the idea of hell, it should be pointed out that the people going there left God out of their lives all of their lives and God just made the situation permanent. If anything, hell is a compliment to a person's freedom of choice. G. K. Chesterton wrote, "Hell is God's great complement to the reality of human freedom and dignity of human personality."

It should also be pointed out that the punishment is so great because the crime of rejecting Christ is so great. Let me tell you the punishment for a crime, and you tell me the crime: a $10.00 fine; a year in jail; five years in jail; life imprisonment; death. If you believe in justice and that punishment should be commensurate with the crime, you will see that the greatest crime in the universe is rejecting Jesus Christ.

Perhaps the most important fact about hell is that no one, absolutely no one, has to go there. Christ died to keep everyone out of hell. All anyone has to do is trust in Him and His death on the cross as the payment for their sins, and that individual can and will escape eternal hell.

Hell? No!

In a heated debate on the floor of the United States Senate, one senator once went into a tirade and, at the climax of his debate, he pointed at his opponent and said, "You can go to hell!" The offended senator immediately jumped to his feet and said to the chairman, who was the Vice President, "Did you hear what he said? Did you hear what he said?" The Vice President, John Garner, pounded his gavel and replied, "Yes, but I looked it up in the books, and you don't have to go."

My friend, you don't have to go. Jesus Christ died to pay for your sins. All you have to do is trust in Him.

CHAPTER 20

DEFINITIONS, SUMMARY STATEMENTS, AND KEY PASSAGES

Believers should be able to define or succinctly summarize the major doctrines and show where they are taught in the Bible. The following definitions, summary statements and key passages are a suggested list for each major doctrine.

> The Definition of God: God is an eternal, spiritual person (1 Tim. 1:17).
>
> The Attributes of God: The major characteristics of God are:
> *Sovereignty:* God is supreme; He rules over everything and has absolute power (1 Chron. 29:11-12).
> *Omnipresence*: God is everywhere present (Ps. 139:7-12).
> *Immutability:* God is unchangeable (Mal. 3:6).
> *Omniscience:* God knows all things actual and possible (1 Jn. 3:20).
> *Omnipotence:* God has the power to bring to pass everything which He wills (Rev. 19:6).
> *Holiness:* God is set apart from sin and His creatures (Lev. 11:44).
> *Righteousness:* God always acts in accordance with the law of right, which is within Him (Ezra 9:15).

Graciousness: God is loving, merciful, and kind (Ps. 116:5).

The Trinity: There is one God, but in the unity of the Godhead, there are three eternal and coequal persons, the same in substance (Deity), but different in subsistence (Mt. 28:19).

God the Father: God is the spiritual Father by adoption and by regeneration of all those who put their faith in Jesus Christ (Gal. 3:26).

Jesus Christ: Jesus Christ is the God/Man who died for the sins of the world and bodily arose from the dead (Jn. 1:1, 14; Gal. 4:4; 1 Cor. 15:3-4).

Propitiation:	Because Christ died as a substitute for man's sin, God's wrath and justice are satisfied, and therefore man can be saved (1 Jn. 2:2).
Redemption:	Because Christ died as a substitute for man's sin, man's sin has now been paid for so that man can be set free from his sin (Titus 2:14).
Reconciliation:	Because Christ died as a substitute for man's sin, man's state of alienation from God is changed so that man can now be saved (Rom. 5:10).

Holy Spirit: The Holy Spirit is the third person of the Triune God (Acts 5:3, 4) who regenerates (Titus 3:5), indwells (1 Cor.

6:19), seals (Eph. 1:13), baptizes (1 Cor. 12:13), and enables the believer to obey the Word of God (Eph. 3:16).

> *Regeneration:* At the moment of conversion, the Holy Spirit imparts new life to the believer (Titus 3:5).
>
> *The Baptism of the Holy Spirit:* At conversion, Jesus Christ and the Holy Spirit place the believer into the body of Christ (1 Cor. 12:13).

Inspiration of the Scripture: God superintended human authors so that, using their personalities, they recorded His Word without error (2 Tim. 3:16; 2 Pet. 1:20-21).

Dispensationalism: Dispensationalism is the theological view that God has used different programs to accomplish His purpose (Eph. 3:2; 1:10).

Dignity of Humans: People are created in the image of God and thus have a capacity for holiness and personality (Gen. 1:26; Eph. 4:24; Col. 3:10).

Inherent Sin: Every descendant of Adam inherited the Adamic, corrupt, depraved, sinful nature (Eph. 2:3).

Individual Sin: Every human either intentionally or unintentionally commits personal sins, which are things contrary to the law of God (Rom. 3:10).

The State of Sin: All humans are under sin (Rom. 3:19). Sin: Sin is the lack of conformity to God and His law, either in state, disposition, or acts (Rom. 3:23).

Salvation: God saves individuals from the penalty of sin when they trust His Son Jesus Christ; God is in the process of delivering them from the power of sin in this life and will ultimately deliver them from the very presence of sin (Eph. 2:8; Jas. 1:21; 1 Pet. 1:5).

The Gospel: The gospel is that Christ died for our sins and rose from the dead (1 Cor. 15:1-8).

Regeneration: When people trust Christ, they are given new life (Titus 3:5).

Justification: When people trust Christ, God declares them righteous (Rom. 3:24).

Reconciliation: When people trust Christ, they are reconciled to God (Col. 1:21).

Sanctification: God positionally, progressively, and ultimately sets believers apart to Himself (2 Thess. 2:13; Jn. 17:17; 1 Thess. 4:17).

The Universal Church: The universal church is the spiritual organism composed of all saved people from Pentecost to the Rapture (Mt. 16:18).

The Local Church: The local church is a group of baptized believers organized to do God's work and will (Acts 14:23).

An Ordinance: An ordinance is an outward symbol of a spiritual truth commanded by Christ to be performed by the church (Baptism—Mt. 28:19; The Lord's Table—1 Cor. 11:23-32).

Angels: Angels are an order of beings that God created, some of which serve Him and others, and some of which serve Satan (Heb. 1:14; Mt. 24:41).

Satan: Satan is an angel who fell and led other people away from the service of God (Ezek. 28:13, 14; Isa. 14:12-15).

The Rapture: The Rapture is the supernatural taking away of all church saints before the Tribulation (1 Thess. 4:13-18; Rev. 3:10).

The Tribulation: The Tribulation is a period of judgment lasting seven years and covering the whole earth, which will precede the Second Coming of Jesus Christ (Mt. 24:4-14, 29, 30).

The Second Coming: The Second Coming of Jesus Christ will be Christ's literal, physical return after the Tribulation and before His reign on the earth (Mt. 24:29-30).

The Millennium: The Millennium is the 1,000-year rule of Jesus Christ on the earth (Mt. 25:31; Rev. 20:1-3).

Immortality: All humans have unending existence after death (believers go to be with the Lord—Phil. 1:23; 2 Cor. 5:8; unbelievers go to hell—Lk. 16:19-21, then the Lake of Fire—Rev. 20:11-15).

Heaven: Heaven is a place where all children of God will spend eternity with their heavenly Father (Jn. 14:1-6; Rev. 21, 22).

Hell: Hell, and later the Lake of Fire, is the place of torment for all those who do not trust Jesus Christ in this life (Rev. 20:14).

CHAPTER 21

HOW MUCH DO YOU KNOW?

When I became the pastor of the Church of the Open Door in downtown Los Angeles, the first series I did on Sunday evenings was on basic Bible doctrine. After I concluded the series, with fear and trembling, I gave the congregation an exam. I had no idea how the congregation would respond, as they had come to the service expecting a sermon, only to receive a test instead. To my delight, they were overjoyed. Many requested that I do something similar again.

Now that you have read this material on doctrine, how much do you know? The following is the test I gave my congregation after listening to the Bible doctrine sermons. To take the exam, check whether or not you think each statement is true or false. Later, pick one of the multiple-choice answers that is given. Following the exam is a list of the answers. Then, there is a suggestion about how to evaluate how well you did.

    T__ F__ 1. God is an eternal, personal spirit.
    T__ F__ 2. The Bible teaches that there is one God who exists in three persons.
    T__ F__ 3. The Trinity was not complete until Christ was born.
    T__ F__ 4. God the Father has a body.
    T__ F__ 5. Jesus is 100% God and 100% man.
    T__ F__ 6. The Holy Spirit is a power.

Relating Doctrine To Daily Life

T__ F__ 7. The Bible contains the Word of God.
T__ F__ 8. Inspiration is the recording of truth.
T__ F__ 9. God's program has not changed.
T__ F__ 10. "Created in the image of God" means that we have a body, soul, and spirit.
T__ F__ 11. Every part of humans has been affected by sin, and, therefore, they are unable to respond to God.
T__ F__ 12. I am guilty because Adam sinned.
T__ F__ 13. Salvation is past, present, and future.
T__ F__ 14. Salvation is by faith in the death and resurrection of Jesus Christ.
_____ 15. Justification is a) imputed righteousness, b) imparted righteousness.
_____ 16. Sanctification means a) a second blessing, b) eradication of the sin nature, and c) being set apart.
_____ 17. Progressive sanctification is accomplished by a) the Word, b) chastisement, c) obedience, d) all of the above.
_____ 18. The ordinances of the church are a) baptism and the Lord's Supper, b) elders and deacons, c) evangelism and edification
_____ 19. It is possible to communicate with a) elect angels, b) demons, c) neither, d) both.
_____ 20. After Christ returns to the earth, a) He will take us to heaven, b) He will reign on the earth for 1,000 years.

Answers: 1-T 2-T 3-F 4-F 5-T 6-F 7-F 8-T 9-F 10-F 11-T 12-F 13-T 14-T 15-b 16-c 17-d 18-a 19-d 20-b

If you got 15-20 correct, you have faithfully read these chapters and retained much of what you read. Or, it may mean you knew something about basic Bible doctrine before picking up this material.

If you got 10-14 correct, you must study. Perhaps you need to reread the chapters dealing with the questions you missed.

If you got less than ten correct, you are a sitting duck for confusion or a cultist!

The test you just took is a simple, basic exam. If you got a good score, don't get too proud. The questions could have been much tougher. If you did poorly on such a simple test, you lack knowledge of basic Bible doctrine. You need to learn. Perhaps you should reread this material or study the particular chapters in which you are weak. You also need to attend a Bible-believing, Bible-teaching church to learn the basics and the advanced teachings of the Word of God. To a great degree, this material is milk, though some of it could be classified as meat. You need to drink all the milk and eat all the meat of the Word of God.

About The Author

G. Michael Cocoris is a gifted communicator. He can make even complicated subjects simple, clear, and practical. His breadth of experience has allowed him to relate to a wide range of audiences.

Michael received a Bachelor of Arts degree from Tennessee Temple University, a Master of Theology degree from Dallas Seminary, and a Doctorate of Divinity from Biola University. He traveled the United States for over a dozen years as a speaker. He has also been a seminary professor, visiting lecturer, and world traveler, including hosting tours to Israel and China.

Michael has pastored three churches, including a rural church when he was in seminary, an urban church, the historic Church of the Open Door, first in downtown Los Angeles and later in Glendora, California, and a suburban church, the Lindley Church in Tarzana California, a suburb of Los Angeles. While at the Church of Open Door, he had a daily radio broadcast.

Michael has written numerous magazine articles, mainly for *Biblical Research Monthly*. He has authored a number of books, including *Seventy Years on Hope Street, A History of the Church of the Open Door*; *How To Live A Biblical Spiritual Life, Clarifying the Confusion*; *Repentance, The Most Misunderstood Word in the Bible*; *Evangelism: A Biblical Approach*; *The Salvation Controversy*; *Lordship Salvation: Is It Biblical?*; *The Books of the Bible, the Subject, Structure, Situation, and Significant Verses of Each Book*; *Psalms, A Song for Every Situation, Each Summarized on One Page*; and *Counseling Theories, A Biblical Evaluation*. In addition, he was a contributor to The *NKJV Study Bible* and *Nelson's New Illustrated Bible Commentary*.

Michael is the pastor of the Lindley Church in Tarzana, California. He and his wife, Patricia, live in Santa Monica, California.

www.ingramcontent.com/pod-product-compliance
Lightning Source LLC
Chambersburg PA
CBHW071641080526
44586CB00013BA/1073